PEER MANAGEMENT

Dr. Allakka Nanda Dash, a senior officer with CISF, belongs to 1988–89 batch of Civil Services (UPSC). She has a Ph.D. in Political Science and a BJMC degree, and is a Jyotish Alankar in Vedic Astrology (from Bharatiya Vidya Bhavan, New Delhi). She has published many books under her two pen names Meena Nanda and Meena Devayani Nanda. She has also published works of fiction, poems and short stories in Oriya language under her maiden name Allakka Nanda. Her published works are:

1. *Boss Management*
2. *A Handbook on Stress Management*
3. *Youth Eternal: Tantra for Vim, Vigour and Vitality*
4. *Sex is not a Sin: Tantra for Healthy Sexuality*
5. *Once in a Blue Moon*

She can be reached through meenananda@sify.com, nanda.alk@gmail.com.

PEER MANAGEMENT

Allakka N D
(Meena Nanda)

MJP PUBLISHERS

Cataloguing-in-Publication Data

Allakka, N D.
Peer Management / by N. D. Allakka. –
Chennai : MJP Publishers, 2009
    xvi, 230 p.; 21 cm.
    ISBN 978-81-8094-055-2 (pbk.)
    1. Socialization – Peer group
    I. Title.
    303.327 ALL MJP 054

ISBN 978-81-8094-055-2   **MJP PUBLISHERS**
© Author, 2009   47, Nallathambi Street
All rights reserved   Triplicane
Printed and bound in India   Chennai 600 005

Publisher : J.C. Pillai
Managing Editor : C. Sajeesh Kumar
Project Editor : P. Parvath Radha
Acquisitions Editor : C. Janarthanan
Editoral Team : B. Ramalakshmi, N. Pushpa Bharathi,
    L. Mohanapriya, Lissy John,
    N. Yamuna Devi, M. Gnanasoundari
CIP Data : Prof. K. Hariharan

To
Pramod Chandra
and
Jyoti Ranjan

PREFACE

All of us conduct our day-to-day life under the influence of friends and foes, who are collectively called peers. Peers are part of that pressure group from which one has no conscious escape. During our formative years we master two basic techniques of "appease" or "fight" in order to cope with peer pressure. However in adult life these two tools often don't see us through as life and relationships are always not divided into watertight compartments of black and white. To handle black and white, grey as well as colourful aspects of peer group politics, we need to sharpen our understanding of psycho-behavioural as well as power game aspects of peership. This calls for peer management skills.

Keeping this perspective in mind, this book has been written as a management supplement both for individuals as well as for the organizations.

In fact like HR management, peer management should be made an integral part of management development studies not only as a tool for damage control but also as a tool for proper utilization of team spirit and synergy of peer groups at the work place and in the societal context. Proficiency in peer management skills is a must for those who are in the field of networking, communication, creativity, production, marketing, consultancy and politics.

Sri Krishna, the master peer manager in the Mahabharata era, had shown many paths for the purpose which if analysed in the right perspective can be understood as the core strength behind the great success of the great epic Mahabharata in the field of value education and life management over such a long period of time. This book draws inspiration from His management techniques.

Peer management being a very important part of life management as well as profession management, this book is aimed at filling a gap in formal education on the subject. It is written for students as well as for professionals and lay persons whosoever is interested in enriching his/her life management and peer management skills by gaining insight into how our peers manage us and how in turn we either fail or succeed in managing them in the right perspective and intention.

Allakka N D

ACKNOWLEDGEMENTS

I am indebted to sage Veda Vyasa who gave us the great epic Mahabharata. The hero of Mahabharata, Sri Krishna, handled his friends and foes in such fascinating manner that it inspired me to develop the models and hypotheses of peer management expounded in this book.

My heartfelt thanks to Ms Kuldeep for word processing the manuscript.

I am thankful to Mr. C. Sajeesh Kumar and MJP people for their enthusiasm in getting this book published.

Last but not the least I am thankful to all my peers, both benevolent and malevolent, for enriching me with different experiences of peer management.

Allakka N D

CONTENTS

PROLOGUE

Peers belong to that group of individuals who provide either a corridor or a culvert or a bridge between the home and outside world—be it the place of work, place of merrymaking or place of spiritual quest.

At times, the peers become our seers and at some other times they become the cause of all our fears. The seers are those whom we count as our friends, philosophers and guides. They not only influence our habits, good or bad, mannerisms, opinions and views, but also affect our most valued reputation, self-esteem, career profile, ethos and values.

The following are two pragmatic sayings pertaining to the Peers.

1. A friend in need is a friend indeed.

2. A person is known from the company (he/she keeps).

The first one tells us that a friend is the one on whom one can count to brave through the rough weather and bad patches of life. If the case is not so then the relationship can be anything else but not friendship.

The second one tells something even more serious, i.e., the company (one keeps and avoids) counts. A human child brought up by animals does not learn to talk and behave like a human being, on the other hand, a pet animal in the company of human beings can imbibe the spirit of fellow feelings, and the intelligent way of communication and companionship, of course only when not used as beasts of burden or tools of amusement. And this is where the crux lies.

Friends or benevolent peers are friends indeed, when we need them, but with the rider that they are not to be used or thought of as our beasts of burden and can't be or rather should not be taken for granted. Peership is a reciprocal and balancing act. Human history is full of anecdotes narrating tales of friends putting everything at stake for each other as well as friends turning into bitter foes after the relationship went sour.

As is in science so is in human relationships—everything is absolutely relative, depending upon the cause and the effect, with the only difference that the causes and effects are at times too subtle and fluid to be detected and reacted upon. And where friends and foes are concerned, the matter becomes more ticklish as at times peers falling in the gray area do and can act like double agents or (to put it mildly) as double-edged swords that can cause grievous injury if one is not careful. So both need careful handling, along with protective sheaths and shields.

In this book, we propose to make a case for that careful handling and prudent use of the sheaths and shields.

In fact, like benevolent peers, the foes or malevolent peers too have their own values as they keep us on our toes and ensure the flow of our adrenaline. Though there is no saying for a foe, we can always coin one— "A foe is a foe who keeps us on our toes and ensures that the adrenaline flows."

Now, who is a foe? Indeed very difficult to comprehend though very easy to define. In simple terms one can say that a foe is not our well-wisher or the foe is the one, who is inimical to our purpose. A foe is the one who not only keeps us on our toes but also at times sucks our blood like a leech and stabs us either from behind or in public. He or she is an individual with a lot of malevolence towards us.

Like friends, foes too have a profound influence upon our behaviour, opinion, career prospects, etc. If the relationship with a friend has a direct impact on these factors, our foes do have an inverse relation on our prosperity and achievements. Like temperature and pressure both play a very decisive and important role in our life.

But many a time, we just take our friends for granted and disregard our foes to our own detriment. Nothing in our formal grooming trains us to adopt a pragmatic and well-defined approach to consciously manage our worldly affairs vis-a-vis our peers. It is simply taken for granted that since human beings are social beings by birth, the instinctive goading should see one through such relationships throughout life.

Perhaps it could be true for a closed society, but in an open prosperous society, where peer groups with the two subgroups of friends and foes do have a tremendous impact, one just can't go by instinct. One is doomed to cut a sorry figure if one does so, as cut throat competition, professional as well as emotional jealousies do have their own effect in permutation and combination like gravitational pulls of planets.

Besides, in a world where resources are limited and opportunities are scarce, one without formal or informal grooming for the purpose is likely to be looked down upon as a simpleton and is bound to feel awkward in formal and informal interactions. In this book, taking cues from Sri Krishna's life, we have put forward hypotheses pertaining to the subject so as to have practical understanding of the rules of the game.

Now, presuming that the reader is well aware of Sri Krishna's identity (for the novices he was the central character around whom the epic of Mahabharat revolved and who narrated Shrimad Bhagavat Gita to his dearest peer Arjuna) and without getting into the dispute as to whether he was really a historical figure or a mythological one or simply a character in a fiction, we propose to draw similies in developing some workable models of peer management, basically to avail the advantage of associative memory without any religious or philosophical superimposition.

In fact, nobody knew better than Sri Krishna how to manage the friends, the foes as well as the chameleons and the fence-sitters with equal ease. But for him we could not have Bhagavat Gita that had helped Arjuna, his friend, in a most distressful yet delicate and decisive moment.

Of course, we are not going to simply replicate his deeds or quotes, rather what we intend to do is to develop hypotheses and models from his way of doing and not doing things and apply them to our circumstances with appropriate modifications as per the requirement of our time and clime.

One has to remember that what Krishna exhibited in all his activities was pragmatism, tact and practical down-to-earth wisdom. Even while handling the worst emotional situations, his actions were guided by his head while his heart never let go of trusting hands.

And this is what we are going to experiment with, i.e., how to be practical, pragmatic, yet loving, caring and mindful of chameleons while handling the peers. An uphill task indeed! But remember the saying, "when you see water flowing uphill it means that someone is repaying a kindness."

In fact, we very often forget to repay the kindness, that our friends bestow on us, at the same time, we don't hesitate to make mountains out of molehills of insults or injuries inflicted by our real and imaginary foes. Besides, many a time, we suffer when our so-called friends change their colour and stab us on our back. And at times, life throws a surprise or two when a sworn enemy shows the magnanimity of extending a helping hand.

It is said that life has its own gait. Likewise, the peer management has its own statics and dynamics. Managing it to one's own advantage to keep up with the gait of life is quite an affair if not a Herculean task. All that one has to do is, tread carefully and remain absolutely mindful of the consequences like the two frogs of a pool that dried up in summer.

To recount the fable, on a scorching summer morning two frogs of one dried pool had set out together in search of another abode and chanced upon a deep well, with ample supply of water and other aquatic animals. One frog suggested they make the well their new home instead of seeking a pool which might prove difficult to find. However prompt came the query from the other frog "But suppose the water of the well gets dried up too, how do we get out of so great a depth?"

In fact, almost all of us are like the first frog, unable to think and feel beyond the present moment. To manage our affairs pertaining to our peers, friends or foes, we need to think beyond the moment and with an eye on the consequences, lest we find ourselves in dried up wells.

The book is meant to induce one to look and think beyond the moment and let the sleeping Sri Krishna inside oneself awaken and handle the peer matters dexterously.

PEER GROUP—INTRODUCTION AND THE HYPOTHESES

The world we know is either I centred or T(hy)/T(hey) centred. From the 'I' centric view, the others are either our contemporaries/compatriots, or competitors and adversaries. Further they could be benevolent or malevolent. Similarly from the 'T(hy)/T(hey)' centric view, one could be a generation apart or a class apart, adding or deleting either of the words benevolent and malevolent as per conveniences.

People

Of the same age

or

same social group

form the

peer group.

And from both points of view where the line of sight gets connected with each other, a circle called peers or "peer group" emerges.

The Oxford dictionary explains the word peer as "People of same age or same social status"—a fascinating word with a unique meaning. Indeed, I call it fascinating because the word does not have an equivalent counterpart to express its meaning in Sanskrit, mother of several Indo-European languages. Besides, while expressing the socio-chronological division, of the people among whom we live, the word "peer" includes expressions like friends and foes.

In other words, it means birds of the same feather, who may or may not be benevolent towards each other. When benevolent, they are counted as friends, well-wishers, and allies. When inimical, they become foes and adversaries. Between the two, the relationship is either a zero sum competition or an equilateral cooperation.

So apart from age and status factor, it is the relationship factor, that adds a third dimension to the word peers/peer.

Further, this word "peer" or "peers" needs extremely careful handling because irrespective of the relative criteria like competition or cooperation, there is always a shadow of expectation or expected pattern of behaviour hanging over it like the sword of Damocles. This is called peer pressure. One either conforms to it or deviates from it. There is no third option.

And though not impossible, it is very difficult to swim against the currents of peer pressure. One may do so at the risk of being branded as "unconventional", "whimsical", "eccentric", etc. which are generally looked down upon as behavioural anomalies.

So with the added fourth dimension, peers can be defined as people of the same age and status group either friendly or inimical towards each other and who are expected to follow a set of particular behavioural pattern befitting their roles and commitment.

Of course, there are odd couples who cut across age and status barrier to befriend or antagonize each other. But in such cases, the third and fourth dimension do remain intact, which means they are either friendly or inimical towards each other and do follow the befitting pattern of behaviour.

In fact, other than our parents and relatives, it is the peer group which exerts the maximum influence on any kind of decision-making process. And since one is known from the company, (that one keeps as well as the company one avoids,) it is very essential that we first understand the four dimensions of peership before understanding the dynamics of our relationship with our peers and the hypotheses/clues for handling such relationships successfully.

THE HYPOTHESES

Let us now structure the four dimensions of peership as four hypotheses and study them in detail for our own benefit.

Four dimensions of peership

Age

Socio-economic status

Relationship

Support system

Hypothesis No. 1

Quality of peerage is directly proportional to suitable appreciation of mutual socio-economic status. (Please keep a note of it as we shall be elaborating on it in our next chapter.)

Hypothesis No. 2

Peerage is directly proportional to time or age factor and varies with the generation gap (when instead of peerage it becomes patronage).

Now coming to the third aspect, we are faced with the word relationship, which is again split into two, benevolent and malevolent, the former turning into harmonious cooperation and the latter turning into bone of contention, striking the note of discord. So our next hypotheses is double aspected.

Hypothesis No.3

Peerage is directly connected with benevolence and is inversely proportional to malevolence.

The fourth aspect revolves around behaviour, that too the manifested or the explicit one, because feelings or thoughts not supported by action are as useless as crocodile tears.

Hypothesis No.4

Peerage is proportional to the omission and commission of timely and much needed action.

Now let us set the ball rolling with a story from the epic Mahabharat which tells us that once upon a time, there were two friends named, Drupada and Drona. The former was a prince of the Panchala kingdom and the latter was a progeny of a poor, learned Brahmin. Both studied together in a Gurukul ashram, the equivalent of a boarding school run by the teacher/preceptor. So, we can say in modern parlance that they were school time buddies, who grew up following the same discipline and regimen under the same preceptor. On passing out, both went their separate ways. Drupada succeeded his father as a king while Drona had to start from scratch as a self-employed person. Obviously the latter had to undergo a severe financial crunch due to absence of any royal patronage or pupil. Disgusted, one day he arrived at his friend's court to seek a few livestocks as a donation to start with. But to his utter disillusionment, his one-time friend refused to accept him as a friend as there was no societal parity between the two. A poor man could never be a befitting friend of a rich man, even if they happen to graduate from the same boarding school was the assertion of Drupada.

Insulted and disappointed, Drona swore to avenge and get even. And thus was born Drupada's arch rival, who, as

Hypotheses of Peerage

Peerage is directly proportional to time or age factor.

Peerage is directly proportional to socio-economic status.

Peerage is directly proportional to benevolence and is inversely proportional to malevolence.

Peerage is proportional to the omission and commission of timely and much needed action.

the story of Mahabharat tells us, with the passage of time formed fresh allies from among his royal pupils and conquered half of the Panchala kingdom.

Of course, that fulfilled the societal and economic requirement of friendship or benevolent peership, even then there after both remained perennially inimical towards each other.

The above is a classic example of a childhood friendship going sour due to utter mismanagement by one party. Perhaps Drupada was never taught at his school the dynamics of peer management. Otherwise, the story of Mahabharat could have been totally different. For Drona could have never looked outside for patronage and Kauravas and Pandavas could not have become his disciples, allies and foes in due course.

If love or benevolence gets paired with hypothesis No. 3, and action is synonymous with hypothesis No. 4, then thought and will are the driving forces behind hypothesis No. 2 and 1 respectively. Though we will study their co-relation, it would be proper to understand the 'why so' logic behind such co-relation between love, thought, will and action.

Love, thought and will are various states of mind, which control or rather are responsible for various actions or inaction of human beings. At times one or all three factors may influence the decision-making and are so intermixed

Four pillars of
human relationship

Love

Thought

Will

Action

with each other in varying degrees that it is very difficult to pinpoint which one was especially responsible for which particular act. Nonetheless these are ever-present invisible factors that do or undo many a time-tested relationship.

In fact these are as pervasive and as universal as the peerage itself. Because except for parent-child-sibling relationship, every other relationship is a combination of peerage and patronage to some extent. And how many emotional, material and strategic deaths do we die day in and day out due to utter misunderstanding of these three intrinsic factors and the sole consequent extrinsic one, i.e., action! How many times do we live to regret a lost or broken alliance due to sheer ignorance of the operating theories and dynamics of peer management hypotheses!

Here I am reminded of a childhood story. Once, two friends came across a bear while picnicing in a jungle. Scared to death, one friend climbed up a tree. Unfortunately the other one did not know how to follow suit. But crisis does compel one to be innovative. So he simply lay on the ground feigning to be dead. The bear smelt him from top to toe and left him untouched thinking him to be dead. (There is an old saying that the bear does not hunt a dead body.) Once the wretched animal left, the friend who had climbed the tree came down and asked his friend, "O dear! did I see the bear whispering something in your ear?"

The other friend replied, "Certainly, the bear advised me not to be friendly with a selfish person."

Needless to say both went their separate ways, never to come together in bonhomie again. The fourth hypothesis and the fourth factor, i.e., timely action governing their equation decided the matter for all times to come.

So even while omitting or committing any act, or for that matter any word, one should be consciously aware of the individual human beings involved in the given situation, the governing extrinsic and the intrinsic factor(s), and the predominant hypothesis acting as the umpire to weigh the events in one way or the other. Whether one succeeds in salvaging or ends up rummaging through the wreckage depends upon how effectively one handles one's finding or judgement vis-a-vis the above factors.

In this book as already stated we develop models for the hypotheses and the factors stated earlier, selecting events from the great epic Mahabharat specially which have something to do with Shri Krishna. Based on these micro models we then attempt to build macro models to apply as well as verify our factors and hypotheses for their universal as well as individual applications.

However, while applying the models and hypotheses, one should not ignore the existence of deviations and wherever possible one should not hesitate to modify or restructure the rules of the game to one's specific advantage. Because the caveat here is, "Change is the constant factor in any relationship, and eventualities carry no more

Change is the
constant factor
in any
relationship,
and
eventualities
carry no more
premium than
the
providentiality.

premium than the providentiality." In fact events are always in so much a transient state as are the human feelings that nothing and nobody can be taken for granted. With time everything changes and failure to adapt to such changes results in disillusionment and ennui. The purpose of peer management and life is to retain the upper hand and have some control over these two.

So the thoughts shared in this book should be used to one's best advantage with as much dexterity and discretion as are required for mastering any other management tool minding the brakes of caveats at their rightful space, since the basic purpose of peer management is to expand one's sphere of influence and weave a network of communication that would see one through both dark and bright phases of life. It is always better to get wise at foresight than regret at hindsight. So read on.

BENEVOLENT PEERS

Every human being irrespective of his/her place of birth remains unaware of any kind of relationship until one reaches the age of five. Before that, one instinctively needs the patronage of elders: be they the parents or anybody else who takes the responsibility of looking after the toddler's basic needs of survival and growth. Once the child learns to walk, talk, and run, the need for playmates and companionship starts manifesting itself in the behaviour. It is the first undifferentiated form of seeking and enjoying a companionship, when an individual, as a child, is yet to remember/discern the malevolence or benevolence in the other human being. In fact the mind as well as the understanding is so fresh that it unconditionally trusts the fellow beings/the experiences with them, such that both sweet and sour are forgotten and forgiven as quickly as they are experienced.

With the onset of the learning process as the memory starts documenting the happenings, one starts differentiating between malevolent and benevolent behaviour with observations and instinct. The survival instinct makes one feel comfortable in the company of the benevolent ones and compels one to be watchful of, and in extreme cases to be wary of, inimical ones, that could be threatening in any way.

MY CAMP VS. OTHER'S CAMP

By the age of eight, the division of **my camp** and the **other camp** starts setting its shop. The entry of the outsiders into either of the camps is regulated to some extent by one's survival instinct but mostly by parental and cultural ambience. People who join or are tentatively enlisted into "my camp" are treated as friends until they are proved unworthy of the camp, whereas for those in the "other camp", osmosis becomes almost next to impossible until and unless something drastically positive or negative happens to change the alignment. This trend set in the pre-teen years guides an individual both consciously and subconsciously in cultivating the adulthood relationship as well.

In this chapter, let us learn the characteristic traits of "my camp" and the "other camp".

CHARACTERISTIC TRAITS OF MY CAMP

The people of "my camp" have two distinct flavours that depend basically on the age factor. The camp of school and college days differs from that of the economically active adult age. The former has the flavour of shared curiosity, raw energy, abstract ideology, and idealized romanticism whereas the latter has matured formalities, practical necessities of survival, procreation, recognition, and self-actualizing factors.

In other words, the hypotheses or governing principles remain the same whereas the factors and flavours of "my camps" keep changing or rather the "my camps" keep re-inventing the factors and flavours as one grows mentally and physically. If the campus day comradeship has the recklessness of youth, the settled working days bring a complex transformation, which is a mix of cooperation as well as competition. The camp however remains nonetheless. The life of Drona, the preceptor of Pandavas and Kauravas of Mahabharat fame, clearly illustrates the above case. Both he and Drupada, the prince of Panchal, belonged to the same camp during their learning/boarding school days. However, as they grew they went separate ways to join the "other camp" that was inimical to each other. In the same way, Drona's disciple Arjuna initially belonged to his camp but after winning the hand of Draupadi, the daughter of Drupada, his camp saw the reverse osmosis which over the years transferred his childhood "our camp" fellows to the other camp. But what remained unchanged in the case of both Drona and Arjuna was their quest for allies to fortify the "my camp". In fact a campless person is regarded as a misfit and is bound to be a failure in the worldly ventures.

For want of a sympathetic and effective "my camp", be it in the form of peerage or patronage, Drona suffered much hardship and ignominy in his life though he had a high profile pedigree and learning at his initial stage of life. And Arjuna along with his siblings went through the hardship caused by the other camp till such time he found "his camp" through marriage alliance with Draupadi and friendship of Krishna.

Thus in our day-to-day life, "my camp" does not matter much socio-economically while growing up but it does make a lot of difference in our adult life.

Perhaps nobody understands it better than sports persons and military persons. For them "my camp" means "Do or die together", "Swim or sink together", "Win or defeat together". In other words, while giving a chance to an individual to be effective, "my camp" also emphasizes

ATTITUDE

      of my camp people

Do or die together

Swim or sink together

Win or defeat together

team spirit. In short, "my camp" says leadership and team spirit should go hand in hand.

WHY FRIENDS ARE FRIENDS: THE PRIME FACTORS

The essence of our preceding discussion must have more or less outlined the reasons as to why friends are friends. However, to make our understanding further clear, it is better to spell those out in clear-cut terms, i.e., sharing, caring and daring.

If we carefully analyse the hypotheses that we had discussed in the preceding chapter, we will find that the hypotheses work well on above three prime factors that draw the dividing line between friendship and foeship. These factors act like bonding or cementing elements. Now let us see what exactly they have to tell us individually and collectively.

SHARING

Like everything else in life, sharing does not happen in vaccum. It happens with certain reference points, the most important of which are

    i. space

    ii. time

    iii. ideology

    iv. event and

    v. goal

Elements of benevolent peers

Sharing

Space

Time

Ideology

Experience

Goal

Caring

Team spirit

Group spirit

Alliances

Daring

Troubleshooting

Adventure

War and love

Defiance

Sharing of Space

Space is that all-pervasive sixth element which while enabling the things and beings to acquire a particular shape or dimension gives them a sense of direction and distance (both length, breadth and depth). It draws the boundary of division as well as alliance. It is the space that initially brings the friends in close proximity in majority of cases. In the age of IT explosion, one can start a friendship in cyberspace or surreal space but eventually one has to either supplement it with real spatial interaction or allow the connectivity to wear out.

In fact crunch as well as expansion of space matter a lot between the friends, especially when growth—whether it be physical, societal, psychological, economic or otherwise—has to take place. Living in the same neighbourhood, growing up in the same campus, working in the same company, sharing one's alma mater, etc. are some of the first and the foremost important criteria of sharing.

It is said that in addition to the physical space, the space in the heart or the mental space matters too. Moreover, this space is more important than the physical space, because the one who gets entrenched in the mental space gets a free ticket to the heart and then a happy joyride to the physical space. In fact, even if the physical space is too narrow to accommodate the favoured one, then one does not mind breaking any number of boundaries to create an additional

FRIENDS

make space

for friends

whereas foes

deprive

one of one's space.

space for the one who has got a gate pass to one's mental space.

Friends make space for the friends whereas foes deprive one of one's space. Mahabharat tells us that Drona took away half of Panchal kingdom and Kauravas deprived Pandavas of their Indraprastha for thirteen years.

Sharing of Time

Time is the least understood yet the most important abstract commodity, which acts as a deciding factor in making, sustaining, or breaking any relationship. For, in our known world, things are regulated mostly by the time factor. And we all, without any exception, allocate our time to events and persons as per our own priority. Accordingly the one in the least priority group gets the least time.

When we give our time to somebody, we are actually giving our attention and presence to him/her. Our mind and our senses and mind suspend every other activity to listen to or to understand the one with whom we decide to share/spend our time. Besides, time with its three divisions—past, present and future—also plays an important role in the process of decision-making. If we have bitter memories of the past, we are reluctant to share our time and space, but if they are warm and positive, they encourage further sharing. Invariably, the past has an effect on the present and future status of sharing almost without exception. But with changing time and clime one does

The old saying,
"a friend in need is a
friend indeed," stands
tall as the most
important factor
governing the sharing
of time.

True friends stand by
us in thick and thin
not only by their
words but also by
their actions and
emotions.

change the attitude towards the sharing factor. However, the saying "A friend in (hours of) need is a friend indeed" stands tall as the most important factor governing the sharing of time.

But since time not only means the "when" factor but also means the "duration" or "for how long", the extent of friendship also varies with the duration factor. Friends are usually tested for their staying and sustaining power. A short-term sharer is regarded only as an "acquaintance".

Sharing of Experience

Experience is the mother of all wisdom. It is also the true barometer for gauging the depth and utility of each relationship. Because experience is the acid/litmus test that can make or mar any equation and relationship. In other words, it is the right action at the right time that sets apart the true friends from the false ones and the chameleons. The true friends stand by us in thick and thin not only by their words but also by their actions and emotions. There are fair-weather friends who hang around at the time of plenty and glory, but come autumn, suddenly all of them remember one or the other vanishing trick, while long-forgotten friends resurface as our saviours.

Shared experiences of war, danger, adventure, crisis and calamity work as stronger bonds than the bonding of shared pleasure and plenty. Also, shared experiences of loss and gain stand as the testimony of friendship and companionship.

EXPERIENCE,
the mother of
all wisdom,
is the true
barometer
for gauging
the depth and
utility of each
relationship.

Sharing the Ideology

If human beings are set apart from other living beings on the ground of speech and intelligence, it is the "ideology" that works both as the binder as well as the divider among the *Homo sapiens*.

Now let us see what an "ideology" is? Ideology is an unconscious belief in an "idea" about one or other aspect of life, nature, and God. The aspects of life include socio-economic, political, and relational side, and the aspects of nature and God need no explanation, for we all know that they are the basis of all our religious groups. In fact, of all the shared "ideas" and "ideologies", the ideas on economy, God, and societal relationship (including sex) are the most important to people who belong to "my or our camp" because they eliminate the factors of suspicion and difference that would otherwise be treated as the symbol of a foe.

People, strangely, live and die for their ideology especially those who are young, emotional and illiterate. Such people are called fanatics who truly believe that their ideology is the best ideology and that the world and humanity is in danger as long as there is any other variety. They take upon themselves the self-imposed burden of making the world a safer and better place by eliminating every other ideology and the followers of those different paths.

In fact, sharing an ideology is a stronger cementing force than sharing space, time and experience. Any insult by

SHARING
an ideology
is a stronger
cementing force
than sharing
space,
time
and
experience.

anybody else to the shared ideology is taken too personally to be ignored.

Sharing of Goals

Shared goals or objectives are the other common points among the benign peers. The goals may vary from economic, political, societal, scientific, and cultural to any other aspect of life.

It is the achievement of the goal, the shared sweating out, shared holding out and shared benefits that justify the membership of one in "our or my camp". In fact while the shared goals of the same camp enhance mutual benefits, they also reduce or deprive the chances of the "other camp" of the same achievements. Without a shared goal, it is very difficult to have a desired degree of cohesiveness that would ensure the "swim and sink together" attitude in the otherwise challenging situations.

CARING

Every human being needs a certain amount of care, especially for fulfilling the basic needs such as food, shelter, clothing, protection against disease and natural calamities. It is also needed for the acquisition of knowledge and technology that affects the quality of economic and other activities. It is needed to attend to procreative, recreational and creative urges like sex, sports, fine arts, etc. The people of "our camp" or "my camp" facilitate the process by extending benign

"Our camp"
or
"my camp"
people extend a
benign support
and care, which tells
us that they care
and we matter to
them.

support and care, which tells us that "they care" and we matter to them. It leaves such a longlasting impact that even long after the needs or events are over, one does not mind recognizing and acknowledging affiliation to the cause, the "camp" and the people. In fact it imbibes what is called the spirit of "team-mate", "room-mate", "work-mate", "class-mate", "school-mate", "college-mate", "course-mate", etc. We can simply call it as the "team spirit", "group spirit", and "alliance spirit". In fact such spirits not only bind people of the same camp but also attract the fans/admirers/sympathizers.

Team Spirit

Team spirit is not simply about sharing the space, time, experience and goal but it is also about tolerance of diversity and appreciation of equally situated fellow beings.

Team spirit is best manifested or explained in a sports or cultural event. In any team-oriented sports event including relay race, what matters the most is the ability to carry everybody else in the same boat knowing fully the strength and weaknesses of each individual, a know-how that compels to avoid or ignore "complexes" and to utilize the assets as well as liabilities to achieve one's pre-decided goal or objective.

Team spirit strives to imbibe the quality of extending a helping hand to the needy members without any underestimation or malevolent purpose. Such display of noble qualities earns the members not only the respect but also the admiration of like-minded people who for some or other reasons are not the formal members of the team.

The Group Spirit

A group is slightly different from a team though both stand for a collective effort at achieving a certain goal. Group spirit can be best explained in terms of project management or in terms of business houses with clusters of goals that hold people together for various economic and other reasons. It is a bigger pool of synergy that is available to the "our group" or "my group" people.

Alliances Spirit

The war situations as well as marriages are examples of alliances, i.e., caring for each other's interest. The friends ally with each other to protect their common interest and to ward off encroachment that would result in loss. Alliances like marriage have certain compensatory obligation in case one wants to pull out or change camp, i.e., divorce or desert one's partner for one or other reason. Such obligations are meant to discourage shifting of loyalty and commitment.

DARING

The pull of adventure or of the unknown seems to strangely attract human beings, and is the mother of every discovery, invention, philosophy and exploration.

So basically what the "my camp"/"our camp" people try to do while pulling their synergy is to dare to reach a level, or to achieve/accomplish certain objectives like scaling a mountain peak, deciphering the DNA code, discovering a new land mass, inventing radio waves, making an atomic bomb, etc. Daring has its own clusters of goal-oriented groups or sub-camps such as the following.

Trouble Shooting/Crisis Management

Troubleshooters or crisis managers excel only under duress when everybody else throws up their hands in helplessness. They seem to have excess of adrenaline only when a disaster or a crisis or trouble raises its head. And it is this extra iota of energy that brands them as the saviours and the messiah, and is the characteristic of this camp.

Adventurous

The pull of the unknown and the challenge of the insurmountable or unconquerable bind this group of dared evils. They are the bold and the brave who are always looking for God forbidden places to sell their new brand of shoes or are always ready to scale the Everest. They are the people who do trapeze shows in the circus and they are the people who walk across the Niagara Falls balancing a stick between their hands. You will find them in rowing clubs, flying clubs and trekking or mountaineering clubs.

TROUBLESHOOTERS
excel when others
throw up their hands
in helplessness.

ADVENTURERS
frequently change
membership and
hence a light-bonded
my group.

WAR AND LOVE
intensifies the
polarization of the
camps.

DEFIANCE
includes change agents
with an indomitable
spirit.

But adventure is one of the very light-bonded "my group" that undergo frequent membership change and there is not much rivalry with the other camp.

War and Love

These two are the oldest adventures in the world that have created and deleted many a celebrity's name from history. And these are the most fascinating daredevil acts that draw sympathetic as well as critical reactions thereby intensifying the polarization of the camps. This daring is always a zero-sum game and hence is the most dreaded as well as the most admired. It draws the finest as well as the fiercest of basic emotions and instincts from within the human heart and head.

Defiance

It is the rebels and the eccentrics who fall into the category of daring. These are the people who are always, for one reason or the other, at loggerheads with established norms, rules, codes of conduct and the system. They are the revolutionaries, the gangsters, the rebels, the new-era philosophers, etc.

They are the change agents who are not afraid of any negative change and have disenchantment with status quo. They derive a thrill from being on the run or being chased. They are proud and arrogant people with an indomitable spirit that does not even recognize the sky as the limit.

They inspire both awe and fear in the hearts of both their friends as well as their enemies.

TYPES OF BENEVOLENT PEER GROUPS

So far, we have known the factors that justify the friendliness of a friend or the benevolence of "my/our camp". Now let us have a look at different types of friends. It is essential to know the types of classification of friends because the application and success of peer management tools depend upon the group characteristic of the same.

Since we are talking of Sri Krishna's life story as prototype, we divide the friends into following five broad groups.

KRISHNA GROUP

Before we outline the special features of the Krishna group, let us briefly recount his personality and life events for the benefit of those who have not learnt the story. He was born in the dungeon/jail and was the eighth child of his parents who were relatives of the ruler of the Yadava clan republic that had its capital at Mathura (presently in Uttar Pradesh state of India). His maternal uncle, Kamsa, the then ruler was initially very fond of his cousin Devaki. However, due to anti-incumbency sentiment of the populace, Kamsa's public image was depicted as that of a greedy despot who had more interest in imposing heavy taxation that was required to sustain his military powers, than in good governance.

As usual, a section of intellectuals and influential citizens were on the look out for an alternative to the leadership. Since Kamsa suppressed his opponents with an iron fist, it was not an easy job to find a viable replacement. So keeping with the tradition of the time, public opinion was mobilized in favour of change in leadership in future. In the absence of electronics or any other sophisticated mass media, word of mouth or rumour was adopted as the propaganda tool. And it was decided that if the alternative leadership comes from the near ones of the inner circle of the powerful one, then perhaps acceptance would be better, and it would be easier to penetrate the impregnable fortress.

KRISHNA GROUP

* Born leaders
* All rounders
* Broad-minded
* Love-personified
  (with dear ones)
* Revenge-personified
  (with malevolent ones)
* Dependable and
  steadfast
* Withstand peer
  pressure
* Mould public opinion

The most rare and ideal group whose presence enlightens the peer group.

So, Vasusdev, the father of Sri Krishna, was thought of as the most suitable alternative man to provide a worthy progeny who would be an all-rounder and who would live up to the political, economic, spiritual and emotional expectation of both the masses and the elite. The rumour mill and grapevine was literally used to fuel the public imagination and a long drawn propaganda and psychological warfare ensued.

Thus against this background was born the man of destiny Sri Krishna whose six elder siblings were killed by Kamsa immediately after their birth. The seventh one survived because of premature delivery. His parents paid the heavy price of spending their youthful conjugal life under house arrest.

Immediately after his birth, Sri Krishna was sent away so that he could grow incognito. However he had to survive many secret attempts on his life during his infancy. But with proper grooming, he grew up to the expectation of all and became one of the most enigmatic, successful and charismatic personalities of his time. In due course of time, he not only challenged the existing orders of the day but also succeeded in eliminating the leadership of Kamsa. But instead of growing arrogant and selfish, he adopted humility and tact as his trademark of leadership. He became a friend, philosopher and guide to those who cared. Instead of becoming a new ruler, he very wisely preferred to be the kingmaker, i.e., the power behind the throne.

From the above narration, the personality traits of Krishna group of benevolent peers must be clear. However, for clarity of thought, let us recount what people like or personalities like Krishna stand for and what they symbolize.

Personality Traits of Krishna Group

❀ They are born leaders.

❀ They have larger-than-life images.

❀ They are all-rounders, i.e., they have understanding of every aspect of life including politics, science and spiritualism.

❀ They neither live in ivory towers nor are they armchair thinkers.

❀ They are moulded as change agents with mass acceptability.

❀ They are practical and are experimentalists.

❀ They believe in success and victory and become successful in their chosen field.

❀ They are broad-minded, i.e., they have the understanding of laws of nature and human psychology.

❀ They are a blend of scientific as well as artistic talents.

❀ They neither look down upon nor look up to anybody for falling back during rough weather. They manage themselves.

- They are inquisitive and have very high Applied Spiritual Quotient (ASQ).

- They do not mind riding the roller coaster of life's events with equanimity.

- They are the first among the equals and are a cut above others.

- They are neither moral nor immoral. They are amoral.

- They are dependable and steadfast.

- They can withstand the peer pressure and mould the public opinion.

- They are very successful in handling their public as well as private life.

- They don't mind changing tactics as per suitability of the situation without letting anybody in their camp down.

  (In fact in the company of such august benevolence, one can let oneself go.)

- They are "Will" personified.

- They are sincere and true to their thoughts, words and actions.

- They are adaptable to changes.

- They are "love" personified with dear ones and "revenge" personified with malevolent ones.

- The word "impossible" does not exist for them.

Among the benevolent peers, the Krishna group is the most rare yet the most ideal one. One needs to be fortunate enough to be in such enlightened company. Such friends demand absolute faith, absolute trust, absolute and unconditional love and in return they won't mind carrying your burden as if it were their own. Such peers are self-managed, provided you behave. They are accommodative.

Once we learn about the traits of other groups of friends, we will discuss how these five groups manage each other.

RADHA GROUP

The Radha character does not occupy a prominent place in the Mahabharat epic as such. But it finds a place under the name Vishakha. (It will be pertinent to mention here that the epics like any other mystic writing have manifold meanings and the characters do have multiple names/ synonyms). So Radha is also known as Vishakha—the sixteenth asterism or nakshatra of Vedic astrology. (Traditionally, a child born under a particular asterism was given the name after that asterism.)

Vishakha or Radha belonged to that group of children among whom Sri Krishna grew incognito till the age of eighteen. The post-epic literature celebrates Radha as love personified. Radha was an elder contemporary of Krishna who was later married to a maternal uncle of Sri Krishna. She was the childhood sweetheart of Krishna and was his companion in mastering the art of dance and music.

She was a rebel who defied gender bias and societal taboo in listening to her heart and feelings. She dared and shared in the company of Krishna so much so that it reached the height of self-actualization. Of course, they went their separate ways once Krishna left for Mathura to fulfil his predestined duties of changing the leadership. They were playmates and love-mates, and once the actions of life sent clarion calls they let each other go by giving unconditional space and time without being possessive and jealous. Both belonged to two different economic strata. Krishna belonged to the martial ruling clan whereas Radha was a cowherdess or a member of Vaisya/business community that depended upon animal husbandry and dairy products for their livelihood. Radha's parents were leaders in that particular group in that particular place.

Personality Traits of Radha Group

* They are reliable companions.

* They are the invisible pillars of inspiration behind every visible successful peer.

* They are the epitome of trust.

* They are the source of unconditional love and support.

* They are the defiants who refuse to go by artificial societal restrictions if it clashes with the dictates of their heart.

RADHA GROUP

* Love personified

* Reliable companions

* Invisible pillars of inspiration

* Epitome of trust

* Source of unconditional love and support

* Emotional but not calculative

* Have an elusive aura and intrinsic values

A rare group of peers whose USP is humility and love and are the best friend material.

- They are the simple-minded people who are not very calculative about gains in return for their emotional support.

- These people are not very ambitious but have an innate understanding of others' responsibilities and ambitions.

- They are capable of going beyond mundane aspects of life.

- They are capable of achieving self-actualization through love and devotion and so they become the centre of attraction.

Like the Krishna group, Radha group is also a very rare group of peers whose USP is humility and love. And in a world where majority takes pride in arrogance and is afraid of love in its true sense, this group of benevolent peers has that rare and elusive aura and intrinsic values in search of which people run to spiritual mentors or change one love-partner for the other.

SUDAMA GROUP

Sudama was the progeny of a poor Brahmin, the highest caste at that time of market economy, who studied together with Krishna in the same Gurukul/Ashram (the modern age equivalent of a boarding school).

For the uninitiated, it is better to mention here that though regarded as the highest of all four castes, the Brahmins were not allowed to amass wealth. Their main vocation was—teaching, research, metaphysics, spiritual priesthood, medicine, astrology, assistance in administration and begging. Teaching included military training, spiritual training, astrological training, literary training, and medical training. However, keeping with the traditional economy everybody was expected to be self-employed. So, many used to run boarding schools where children of all the three upper castes were admitted for proper and suitable education keeping in view their future vocation in mind.

So, Sudama and Krishna were boarding schoolmates. Sudama was a poor Brahmin's progeny who had no certain future and no inherited prosperity to fall back on, whereas Krishna was a proverbial pedigree child who had a whole political system in waiting at his beck and call. Poles apart indeed.

Once they passed out and went their separate ways, Krishna established himself in his unique style in the western coast of India (Dwaraka) and ensured all kinds of prosperity for his clan/kingdom and his kith and kin, whereas Sudama, due to the lack of proper will power and entrepreneurship, languished in poverty and ignominy till his wife forced him to seek favour from his schoolmate Krishna.

Personality Traits of Sudama Group

❀ They are contemporaries from different economic strata.

❀ They are neither strong willed, nor born leaders.

❀ They are not very successful in economic endeavour.

❀ They don't live up to anybody's expectation.

❀ They are failure personified.

❀ They are not very enterprising.

❀ They lack severely in self-confidence.

❀ They need support to stand up and make some meaning out of their life.

❀ They are neither scientific nor artistic.

❀ They look up to somebody for inspiration.

❀ They can neither mould public opinion nor inspire mass following.

❀ They can't see through words and events.

❀ For them, life is a constant struggle for survival.

❀ They are neither innovative nor adaptable.

❀ They don't know how to regain their lost glory.

❀ They are steadfast in their loyalty.

This is the most ordinary and the most prevalent group of peers. We can say this group constitutes fifty per cent of the mass. They are the common people who need scapegoats to blame for their failures and who also need a saviour to remain afloat. Though educated, they are not very good either at worldly affairs or at spiritual endeavours.

SUDAMA GROUP

* Lack self-confidence

* Not very ambitious

* Look up to somebody for inspiration

* Not innovative

* Struggle hard for survival

* Good followers

* Lack charisma

The most prevalent peer group (the mass) who need a saviour to remain afloat.

They lack charisma, effort and determination to rise above mediocrity. But this group has a pseudo pride in its potential and takes time to repose its faith and trust in others. They are not known to have any understanding of love. But once saved, they make good followers. They are found everywhere cutting across socio-economic-political-caste-religion barriers. They are the common ordinary people called "the masses".

ARJUNA GROUP

To recount the life story of prototype of this group, we again have to turn back to the story of Mahabharata.

Arjuna, the famous warrior, was the third child of Pandu, the ruler of the Kuru clan (whose capital was in Hastinapur, around the modern Meerut in Uttar Pradesh state of India) from his first wife Kunti. He was not born through the natural process of sexual union of his parents but was created through an alternate mode of procreation that used Mantra Shakti or sound energy (This technology is lost now). He grew up to be the best archer and was declared to be the most proficient warrior of his time by his preceptor Drona. He had five other siblings, one of whom namely Karna was born to his mother again through Mantra Shakti prior to her marriage and hence was abandoned by her. (Karna was brought up by the royal charioteer). He lost his father during his childhood and along with his brothers and the widow mother had to depend upon his paternal uncle for food, shelter, clothing and education. Being third among his own siblings, he had no chance of becoming a king himself even though his own eldest brother, Yudhisthra had to struggle a lot to get any inheritance from his cousins whose visually challenged father had ascended the throne after the untimely death of Pandu.

Arjuna had to fight a war against his would-be father-in-law Drupada prior to his marriage to Draupadi to repay the fees of his preceptor Drona in the form of a kingdom. And much later he had to fight along with his brothers against his own preceptor Drona and paternal cousins to claim his inheritance of which he and his siblings were deprived through duplicity and cunningness. He was fortunate enough to have the benevolent peership of Krishna, preceptorship of Drona and marital alliance with Panchali or Draupadi, the daughter of Drupada, the King of Panchala. It is Arjuna for whom Srimad Bhagavat Gita was spoken by Sri Krishna to pull him out of pre-war depression and mood swing.

Personality Traits of Arjuna Group

- ❀ They are bold and brave.
- ❀ They are goal-oriented.
- ❀ They have tremendous power of mental concentration.
- ❀ They are ambitious and hard-working.

ARJUNA GROUP

* Good learners
* Versatile and multi-talented
* Tremendous power of concentration
* Goal-oriented, ambitious and hard-working
* Good strategists but lack eye for details and fine-tuning
* Cut-throat competitors

Constitute one-fourth of the mass who have a burning desire to excel in whatever they do.

❈ They are at times prone to mood swing, anger and other negative emotions.

❈ Due to overdrive, they at times suffer from burning out and exhausted adrenaline syndrome.

❈ They are successful leaders as well as followers in their chosen field.

❈ They are good learners.

❈ They are versatile and multi-talented.

❈ They are ruled both by the head and the heart.

❈ Though they are good strategists, they lack the eye for details and fine-tuning.

❈ They are basically macro-managers and lack desirable cunningness to see through the traps.

❈ They are dependable and steadfast.

❈ Though prone to short temper, they are loyal and committed.

This group constitutes about one-fourth of the mass. They are the second-rung leaders who are efficient at executing directions. They are cut-throat competitors who have this burning desire to excel in whatever they do. They are not afraid of competition and do express grudging admiration wherever they meet their match.

DRAUPADI GROUP

Draupadi, the adopted daughter of Drupad, was adopted along with her brother Dhristadyumna after proper initiation. Drupad had another adopted son who was initially the daughter (Amba) of Benaras (Kasi) King. After the sex change process, she had adopted the name Shikhandi (the eunuch) to seek revenge upon Bhisma, the grand old patriarch of Kauravas and Pandavas. Drupad wanted to get even with Drona, who was once his childhood friend. So to have a worthy progeny he had arranged for a Yagna/fire sacrifice and both Draupadi and Dhristadyumna were adopted, a boy to fight the military prowess of the enemy and a girl to get a powerful ally through marital bond.

Like her father Drupad, Draupadi too was a unique person, who knew the political purpose of her princessdom. She had accepted the aim and ultimate justification of her existence with a very rare and highly admirable attitude that is not generally found in women of any genre. She was ambitions, revenge, pride, arrogance, power, commitment and friendship personified in a very rare combination.

Sri Krishna was her friend, philosopher and guide. He suggested to her that she select Arjuna as her groom, who qualified the critical test of hitting the eye of a moving fish by aiming at its reflection below. Under strange circumstances, she came to become a common wife of

Arjuna and his four brothers—the only polyandrous princess in known literature/history. Because of the political rivalry between her husbands and their cousins (Kauravas), she was humiliated in a game of dice. She and her husbands had to suffer the life of ignominy and wretchedness of vagabond wanderers when Yudhishtra lost the kingdom again in a game of dice.

It took about thirteen years of wandering and an additional 18 days blood bath of Mahabharata war to regain the lost glory and dignity. Though there were several factors that precipitated the war, it is said that apart from the kingdom it was the exceptional beauty, pride and arrogance of this lady, (her royal highness Draupadi who was famous for her cascading hair, stunning looks and acid tongue) that was the main apple of discord.

Personality Traits of Draupadi Group

❀ They are ambitious and have no pretension about it.

❀ They are arrogant and never mind calling a spade a spade.

❀ They are very clear about the mission in their life.

❀ They are very sure of themselves.

❀ They are emotional as well as calculative.

❀ They have the strength of the mind, spirit, and body.

DRAUPADI GROUP

* Ambitious and arrogant

* Have a clear mission

* Emotional as well as calculative

* Goal-conscious

* Source of inspiration

* Most admired and most hated

* Good strategists

Power behind the movers and shakers

❀ They fight for a cause and are extremely goal-conscious.

❀ They are dependable and committed.

❀ They can match the Krishna group in strategy and adaptability.

❀ They are the most admired but the most hated at the same time.

❀ They don't mind encouraging destruction of the old order for getting even.

❀ They are brave enough to tread the difficult terrain in search of their goal.

❀ They have the understanding of love and friendship.

❀ They can inspire people to take up alliance for a cause.

❀ They are the overt/covert cause behind many a startling effect.

This group constitutes what in artistic terms is called the source of inspiration. They are the people who need not fight themselves, but for whose honour a thousand would die wilfully. They themselves are neither the destroyers of the old order nor the harbinger of any revolution but they are the intrinsic and the extrinsic cause. They can inspire unity, and can cause split. They are the power behind the movers and the shakers.

MANAGEMENT TOOLS OF SRI KRISHNA

Since the friends are of five types including the Krishna type, let us study the management tools of Sri Krishna under five heads with respect to the hypotheses we have studied in the earlier chapter. Sri Krishna was famous for two gadgets or tools in managing his interpersonal relationships.

One was a flute, and the other was a discus (Sudarshana Chakra). The flute made him dear to his childhood friends. In adulthood it helped him in winning the hearts of the admirers as well as worked as a recreational tool for stress management. Among the benevolent peers the flute acted as a symbol of love, affection, understanding, entertainment, and devotion. So much so that it became an inseparable part of his personality. Playing the flute was an informal and soft way of managing the friends from the core of the heart.

The discus of course was a tool for taming the foes. It is a circular weapon, which was controlled by his mind, and like a boomerang always returned to him after accomplishing the assigned task.

Now let's look at the formal and hard facts of the managerial skills that Sri Krishna had acquired by using the musical instrument and the weapon as his peer management tools, which is not everybody's cup of tea.

SELF-MANAGEMENT (MANAGING KRISHNA GROUP)

For the Krishna-group people, the best peer and the worst foe is found in their own personality. If they are not competent and dexterous in managing themselves, they can create havoc for themselves as well as for the others.

Throughout the story of Mahabharata, we find Krishna handling himself in a perfect manner, his main assets being his self-confidence, strong will power, intelligence power of love and sense of humour. He never allowed anybody to take him for granted nor did he take anybody else for granted. This can be illustrated with the following little anecdote. As a child he was a famous prankster and had an insatiable greed for fresh cream. (It is said that he was born with an awakened Kundalini and was aware of this fact even as a child because of which he could counter many an attempt on his life). This earned him the nickname of the "cream thief" so much so that the cowherds would complain to his foster mother about his habits. Being fed up with this, one day his mother tied him to a tree. And while he was complying with the punishment, another attempt on his life took place. He not only had to defend himself by destroying the attacker but also had to run to inform his unhappy mother. And he could do that by carrying the uprooted tree along with the rope to the utter disbelief of his mother and the company. Thus it is clear that he believed in the principle "self help is the best help, and self defence is the best defence".

Krishna's Management Tools

Flute	Discus
Love	Confidence
Understanding	Go-getter
Entertainment	Commanding
Devotion	Determination
Optimism	Goal

The sense of humour displayed by Sri Krishna is legendary. Even while negotiating peace on behalf of the Pandavas in the court of Kauravas, he displayed such sense of humour that the enemy camp which had planned to put him under house arrest was caught unawares giving him a chance to escape. This acute sense of humour earned him the nickname, Mayavi or the master juggler.

He handled his special status by being a non-conformist. He even went against the established order of worshipping the rain God Indra and substituted him with a more natural, practical and recognizable God, i.e., Govardhana, the hill that supported his foster tribes by providing pasture, fruits, timber, water and other natural resources. Ever since the vedic religion that revolved around Indra lost its sheen and with time the new religion that identified with the symbolic hill, gained popularity woven around the alluring personality of Krishna. The Krishna consciousness movement like ISKCON are the echoes of appreciation for that non-conformist man's actions.

In his life-time, Krishna had no illusion about the nature of things, beings and relationships. He knew who loved him selflessly, who had selfish love, who was deceptive, who was reliable, who needed help, who needed offence, and who was trustworthy. This extreme awareness made him use discrimination tactfully, as a result of which he was never caught unawares by anybody's deception. His only failure was finding a worthy successor from among his kinsmen. As a result, the science and art forms that he had understood and mastered got lost with him.

His sense of time and space was very practical. What is to be done and where to be done, and to what extent it can be done were the questions he handled dexterously to claim victory under any circumstance. He knew when it was time to fight, when to flee, when to enjoy, when to oblige, when to help, when to withdraw, when to pretend and when to be one's own self.

Though there was no match for him, he was best handled by Radha and Draupadi, and to some extent by Arjuna. Radha handled him with the tool of unconditional love, Draupadi used absolute friendship and Arjuna was a reliable follower and a colleague. Radha got the essence of him. Draupadi got his best friendship and commitment and Arjuna got his grooming philosophy and counselling. They in fact had the best essence of the flute and discus. All the rest could not get that much benefit.

MANAGING THE RADHA GROUP

The Radha-group people are as non-conformist and as self-willed as the Krishna-group people. But their driving force is the emotion of love. We may call it **Love Quotient**. The Radha-group people are partly self-driven, and partly other driven—the other being a specific person or a group of people. Though self-willed, they need an anchor unlike Krishna-group people, who are self-anchored.

Like the Krishna group, the Radha group also has that mysterious 'X' factor which makes them a cut above—but unlike Krishna group these people are not very ambitious. So how do they handle themselves and how did Krishna handle them (or how did the Krishna group people manage them)?

In the main story of Mahabharata, we don't find much importance given to Radha or to people like her. However, in the post Mahabharata literature especially after the Buddhist era somehow love quotient gained recognition. So from the portrayal of Radha as a woman married to somebody else, yet developing the bond of love with another man was glorified as a quest for self-actualization. In other words, Radha-group people may or may not be very wise, skilful or experts in accumulating either worldly wealth or great name and fame for themselves, but they have a very powerful palpating heart firmly planted inside their chest that rules their head. They don't mind putting everything at stake for "love" and their self-management tools are trust, benevolence, sacrifice, patience, courage, determination, intense emotions, willpower and all the other allies of love. Surprisingly these people are not possessive. They believe in giving space to the other and to themselves. They know when to hold a person and when to let them go. This gives them the much envied independence of will and a stranger's value. They are the best friend material.

Krishna-group people have clear understanding and appreciation of these qualities of Radha group. They manage them by not only reciprocating the feeling but also by gently guiding and anchoring them. Because the Radha-group people are extremely sensitive to negative feelings, they become crest fallen if betrayed. Though courageous and non-conformist, their high love-quotient makes them prone to frustration and anger. Of course gentle anchoring and counselling as well as pampering puts them back on the track. Yet they can cry themselves hoarse when discriminated against.

Since they are very sensitive and intelligent people, they have this acute sense of self-awareness too. They know themselves inside out. This at times lends them a bloated ego which is invariably punctured by Krishna group with tact just to instill that much required down to earth feeling without which the Radha-group people may turn into ego maniacs because of their proximity value to enigmatic Krishna-group people. This countercheck helps them in proper harnessing of their emotional synergy. Being extremely sensible and intelligent, Radha-group people do learn their lessons very fast and make it a point not to repeat their mistakes.

Anecdotes about Radha-Krishna equations mention that one day Radha felt very proud of her love for and proximity to Sri Krishna. At that time, out of love, Krishna was carrying her in his arms. The moment the monster of pride took possession of her, Krishna could sense it and pretending to tumble upon a stone he lost his balance and dropped Radha on the ground. In the process Radha sprained her ankle, but nonetheless she understood what caused her fall. Once bitten, she was twice shy to ever allow pride to take the centre stage vis-a-vis her equation with Krishna.

The same Radha never compelled Krishna to stay back at Vrindavan after puberty. When the call of his life's mission took him to Mathura and thereafter to Dwaraka, Radha neither forced him to stay back, nor begged to be taken along. She stayed back at her own place neither following Krishna's footsteps nor committing her lifelong companionship to him. Indeed, a leader guided by her own mind and heart. Radha group people don't make good followers nor do they allow external imposition of any decision. They decide for themselves. And Krishnas allow them to have their say, for Krishna too never forced her to accompany him in the course of his life's meandering path. We were not sure about Radha's progenies from her marriage to Chandrasena, neither do we have any account of her later life. It was as if she preferred to live a life of self-imposed ignominy. But centuries later, she became famous for her high "love-quotient", as Krishna's companion, and for her source of inspiration for those who seek self-actualization and self-fulfillment through love.

Radha-group people somehow don't get instant fame but are those rare people who are self-actualized in the real sense of the term.

MANAGING THE SUDAMA GROUP

The Sudama-group people are just the opposite of the Krishna group in terms of self-confidence and leadership qualities. They nonetheless are good follower materials. Severely lacking in initiative, they are the target group for all those self-help, motivation fundas doled out by management gurus. But somehow the fellows miss the hint.

Sudama-group people are poor in economic achievements or we can say that their self-help power to improve their own lot is very low. They might inherit their societal status by virtue of their birth, may be well educated but are the worst practitioners of whatever they learn. They are neither good workers nor good managers. They manage themselves by over-using the tool of self-pity and misery. Resource generating through innovative means is just not their cup of tea. Ignominy serves them right. But their highly inflated ego prevents them from seeking help very openly.

They are neither excellent peers nor formidable foes. In fact their lack of enterprise and non-imaginative personality makes them the worst foe. But as a part of peer group, they are neither capable of exerting pressure nor capable of taking the centre stage. It makes them the most easily manageable group.

The Krishna-group people are in fact amused in the company of Sudamas. Though belonging to the same alma mater, somehow Sudamas lag behind in the race of life.

And in the long run when they decide to seek assistance from their peers they turn to the Krishnas for help. And how does a Krishna manage this peer? The answer is by being magnanimous, as Krishnas are very much aware of the fragile and sensitive ego of Sudamas. Their magnanimity is backed with compassion and fellow feeling. It is never grounded or tinted with contempt or underestimation. This is what makes them stand apart in a crowd of Drupadas who under similar circumstances not only hurt the sentiments but also resort to arrogant show of affluence and superiority. This adds to foes whereas magnanimity turns such needy and deprived souls into lifelong fans and followers.

The catch here is the magnanimity coupled with subtle nostalgia and fellow feeling. The Sudamas do acknowledge it a little belatedly, i.e., when the realization dawns upon them. But surprisingly the enterprise and leadership qualities never rub off on them. So from this peer group, the Krishna-group people don't get any competition for primacy. And Sudama-group people are those peers who can never ever change their camp and turn into enemies.

MANAGING THE ARJUNA GROUP

Among the skilled ones, the Arjuna group stands at the top but lack of foresight, balance of mind and strategic thinking makes them stand second in the leadership rung.

They having the mixed trait of Radha, Sudama and Draupadi need a mixed path of management.

If we talk in terms of a simile, the Arjunas would qualify as good actors whereas Krishnas are the producers, directors and scriptwriters. If Krishnas are the CEOs/proprietors then the Arjunas are the production/sales managers. The positive aspect of it is that the Arjunas are aware of this fact. And the negative aspect is that they get lost without the guidance of their friend, philosopher and guide, i.e., Krishna.

The Arjuna-group people manage themselves by excelling in one or more fields of knowledge and skill. At the time of adversity, these skills come handy to them. They prefer to be mobile and are by nature adventurous. Though good at heart, brave and daring, they are not very successful as administrators. Their emotion quotient and skill quotient being almost equivalent, at times both cancel out each other, causing the dilemma of "to be" or "not to be". Though absolutely goal-oriented and ambitious, their mind gets clouded by emotions, as they are not ruthless executors like Krishna-group people. They are single-minded while acquiring skill and knowledge, but are poor crisis managers as their heart rules over their head especially while handling the affairs of human beings. Though brave and bold, they are not rebellious. However, they are good and willing co-workers in case the Krishnas spell out any innovative ideas.

The Krishna-group people take full advantage of these factors while managing this group of peers. Intelligently they eliminate any scope of competition between themselves by forging personal bonds of societal alliances apart from being informal and encouraging. When required to choose, they openly side with the Arjuna group of people, patronize them and groom them for higher purposes of life. But unfortunately the Arjunas are meant only for the mundane world. The higher philosophy of Gita just passes over their head. They are the people who don't reach the level of self-actualization or enlightenment even if the Krishnas try to push them through it. In fact they are the people who have the potential of becoming a Krishna but don't realize it neither are they ambitious enough to achieve it. But the potential forges a natural bonding between both the groups making them confirmed peers who can never turn into foes.

MANAGING THE DRAUPADI GROUP

The female compatriots of Krishna group, Draupadis, are somehow lesser in stature to Radhas but are much above Sudama and Arjuna group. They are the friends of the opposite sex with whom one is comfortable enough to share the personal and professional views about any and everything without having any emotional or sexual entanglement. But they bond with each other through a different level of love, the love for a friend, which is at a

BENEVOLENT PEER—MANAGEMENT SLIDE-BAR

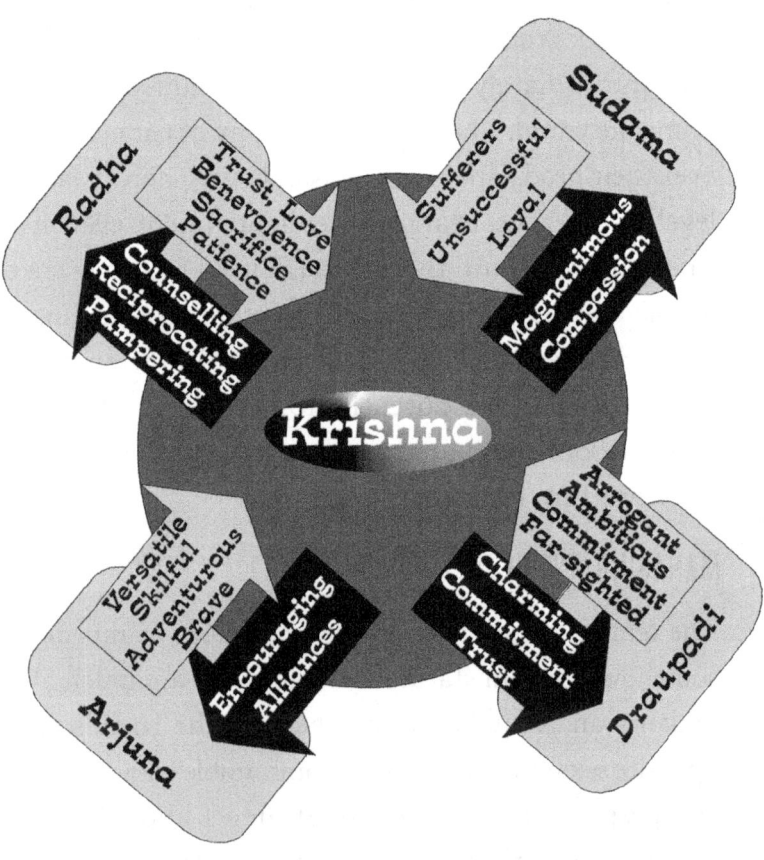

higher level of wavelength of which Sudama or Arjuna group people have no understanding.

Proud and haughty, Draupadis do have the understanding of higher aspects of life but prefer to concentrate on mundane aspects only. Farsighted, sharp, arrogant and ambitious, the Draupadi-group people manage themselves through seer straightforwardness. Diplomacy is not their forte. Though endowed with natural physiological assets, they do not go out of their way to be charming to all and sundry; but in spite of this defence mechanism they have the understanding of love and cameraderie. They win the friendship and confidence of Krishnas by their intelligence and on-your-face attitude. However, these are the qualities that land them in trouble when in unworthy company. They have this cultivated highbrow attitude which lands them in professional as well as personal troubles. But sooner or later with the help of Krishnas they get even with their foes.

There is something very high profile about these people, which is very subtle yet palpating and they are acutely aware of the same. This makes them stand apart from the crowd. It is a rare combination of both attitude and charisma. When taken or misunderstood as an attitude-causing factor, it antagonizes others by inducing a feeling of inferiority complex. The Draupadis have no clue as to how to handle it to their advantage. In fact a little more diplomacy could make them the apple of everybody's eye, but they somehow become the centre of discord.

The Krishna group tackles these people by humbling and charming them with unconditional support. They stand by the Draupadis through thick and thin, taking care not to be critical of their shortcomings. In return Draupadis get the full advantage of Krishna's foresight and premonition as well as intuition. The basis of their relationship is total understanding and trust. It is friendship par excellence because both have the insight of all those factors that turn friends into foes and vice versa.

The practical wisdom learnt from experiences cautions them against any transgression. Though basically belonging to the opposite sex, there is no connotation of sexual attraction between the two groups. In fact they complement and supplement each other so perfectly that both can be taken as mirror image of each other except for Krishna's psychic powers. In fact these inherent as well as acquired powers make Krishnas their saviour during their difficult times.

In fact but for Krishnas, the powerful personalities like Draupadis do not have many peers to depend upon. Even at times their near and dear ones stand helpless spectators letting them suffer the humiliations. But it is the Krishnas who under no circumstances let them down. In fact their commitment defies any logic and is beyond the comprehension of ordinary human beings.

W in
I ntrigue
S ustain
H elp

A ccept
C ounsel
T rust

S erve
W ait
I nspire
M anoeuver

S acrifice
I ncubate
N egotiate
K eep open

Modern Management Skills

MODERN MANAGEMENT SKILLS

Based on Sri Krishna's strategies, certain core points can be elucidated for constructing models for management of friends in modern times. These core points have been placed in four broad groups with acronyms such as (i) WISH (ii) ACT (iii) SWIM and (iv) SINK. Let us study these individually.

WISH

WISH stands collectively for (a) Win, (b) Intrigue, (c) Sustain and (d) Help.

Win

Wise people defeat enemies and win friends.

A famous saying reads "Oh Lord please take care of my friends I will take care of my enemies". This is what the "win" stands for. It is easy to defeat a foe but very difficult to win a friend. Because friends are privy to counselling us and thereby influence our decision-making. The proximity also breeds complexes that add to rivalry and back stabbing. For example, Caesar was assassinated by Brutus in connivance with his heir apparent. Napoleon was let down by his own ministers.

Our model Krishna himself was a sufferer at the hands of his maternal uncle Kamsa. But intelligent as he was, he had learnt the lessons of reality management very early in

Wise people
defeat
enemies
and
win
friends.

his life. The select few whom he chose to treat as his friends were tried, tested and thereafter won over with due efforts by helping them when they had exhausted all other sources. This earned him their lifelong loyalty and eliminated the scope of competition that otherwise usually sooner or later affects the dynamics of friendship.

So while working out strategy for foes, it is essential to win over friends for one's own peace of mind.

Intrigue

People love mystery and have a penchant for guesswork and speculation.

Though we all are born with almost equivalent faculties, the gradual unfoldment of the physical and mental potentialities makes each individual human being unique and different. Among the peers, those who excel in one or other field automatically become the path breakers. But to win over the admiration of friends and to sustain it for a prolonged period of time, one has to develop two different strategies—one to win over; the other to sustain it. The sustenance part is the most difficult one as over a period of time familiarity tends to breed contempt.

So it is very essential to draw a line of demarcation beyond which one has to exercise one's discretion and right to privacy. Though a broad outline of action and reaction can be discussed with calculated casualness, the details should be kept to oneself giving room for guess and

Many a
relationship
dies a
starvation
death
due to
lack of
nurturing.

speculation. It helps in weaving the aura of mystery, intrigue and gives one the status of being somebody different from the herd.

Sustain

Many a relationship dies a starvation death due to lack of nurturing.

All our relationships do follow a natural cycle of inception, growth, blooming, fulfillment, decline and death. Consciously or unconsciously, we let nature follow its own course in most of our interactive relationships. But the relationships with our friends that we really don't want to decline for our own selfish or philanthropic reasons should not be allowed to wither for want of attention and care under any circumstances.

A healthy equation with the friends whom we win over or who gravitate towards us for one reason or the other should always be retained at its best. It is prudent to avoid decline and detachment in such equations, as decline in a relationship may give an unwanted access and scope for the entry of inimical forces that in turn may try to gain undue advantage by either neutralizing or winning over our friends. And a friend once lost is difficult to regain for which one has to start all over again from scratch at times paying added premium.

Help

Lending a helping hand to a friend at the time of need proves to one and all that friends in need are friends indeed.

An old Sanskrit saying defines friends as those benevolent human beings who see through the thick and thin of an individual by ensuring their presence, be it at the time of high fortune or at the time of fall from grace.

When Arjuna and his siblings were going through the rough phase of ignominy—after escaping the death trap of the inflammable cottage at Varnavat gifted to them so maliciously by their Kaurava cousins— it was Krishna who stood by them. His was the brain and the planning that saw them through the ordeal of winning a new ally by forging a marital alliance with Draupadi.

Krishna did it with such fineness that never ever was the regal and fragile ego of Arjuna and his brothers hurt or rubbed in the wrong way. While extending a steadfast and farsighted helping hand, Krishna had ensured not to burden their self-respect with any inkling of being slighted or obliged.

The caveat to remember here is not to brag about the help that one renders and also not to sulk if the obligation goes unacknowledged in any form.

ACCEPTING without being judgemental is the most reliable mantra for gaining sidhi in peer management.

ACT

Act stands for three vital components of long-term benevolent peerage.

'A' for Accept

C for Counsel

T for Trust

Accept

Accepting without being judgmental is the most reliable mantra for gaining sidhi in peer management.

The stepping-stone of benevolent peer management is the acceptance—of course mutual—that tells both the parties that within various variable differences, the existence and prosperity of the one is acceptable to the other.

Friends being privy to many a secret do know the strength and weaknesses of each other. And acceptance of a person with both positive and negative personality traits, kind of affirms not only one's own self-confidence but also reassures the other that destructive criticism and backstabbing is not a threat.

Here one has to remember that acceptance does not mean taking one for granted for good. It simply means standing by somebody without any overt or covert ill feeling for whatever positive and negative attributes that one possesses and exhibits and expecting the same in return.

RIGHT COUNSELLING

at the

right time,

right place

and for

right cause

acts as a catalyst
for effective
peer management.

In simple words, it is simply letting the other person be his or her own self without being critical or possessive.

Counsel

Right counselling at the right time, right place and for right cause acts as a catalyst for effective peer management.

Counselling is that form of peer pressure which guards against negative idiosyncrasies of the individual being.

In fact at indecisive moments, it is the right counselling from the benevolent peers that puts one back on to the right track. At traumatic changeover times, it is the peer counselling that sees one through.

We know that Srimad Bhagavat Gita came ito existence only because of the absolute necessity of peer counselling felt by Sri Krishna while Arjuna was under the influence of an emotional and indecisive mind. Such was the extent of wavering that Arjuna was ready to call off the whole war plan. But for the timely and benevolent counselling by Sri Krishna, the course of the whole Mahabharat could have taken a different shape. Arjuna along with his brothers and supporters not only could have become a laughing stock but also could have been regarded as a weakling by his opponents and foes. Besides, we could not have got the gift of Gita, a book of wisdom.

TRUST,
the pillar of
peerage, bears
the load of
acceptability
and
counselling.
Without trust,
these two are
doomed to
collapse.

Trust

Trust is that pillar of peerage which bears the load of acceptability and counselling, and without which these two are doomed to collapse.

Trust is a very subtle yet effectively discernible element and is basic to any benevolent human relationship. Among the peers, it is that 'X' factor which either encourages or discourages the acceptance and rejection. Trust is a verifiable element that can't be quantified in any scale. However, intuition, action and feedback on the basis of ground reality, helps one verify the trustworthiness of one's own near and dear ones. But it is the direction of trust, i.e., whether it is directed towards self or towards the others, that makes a whole lot of difference.

In fact peers are peers because of the trust factor. Take away the trust factor, suspicion and jealousy make way for themselves and play the role of the spoil sport.

It is a delicate commodity, and if not handled carefully it not only gets shattered but also carries along a whole gamut of relationships to the graveyard.

SWIM

Once you decide to WISH and ACT with a peer then the next logical step is to learn to SWIM with your peer group be it upstream or downstream.

It is not
possible
to manage and
sustain peers
without extending
sincere service
as and when
required, expected
and possible.

The acronym SWIM stands for

S—Serve

W—Wait

I—Inspire

M—Manoeuver

Serve

It is not possible to manage and sustain peers without extending sincere service as and when required, expected and possible.

Service to friends is service to self and society. To serve does not mean to be subservient or to expect returns in cash or kind for a favour done to further a cause. It simply means to assist in planning, resourcing and if possible in executing the ideas and the objectives of the friend(s). It also extends to provide moral, emotional and spatial support when such a support is very much needed.

However, lip service is always seen through and despised. So, when it is beyond one's own capacity and circumstances to be of any use, then an honest admission of it saves one from heart burning, backstabbing and most importantly from breach of confidence and from other collateral damages that cause more harm than good to one's reputation as a person.

Wait

Though time and tide wait for none it is the friendship that waits for friends and occasions to prove itself.

In the race of life, the general tendency is to march ahead without waiting for anybody's gain or loss. However, it is just the opposite when one has to manage the peers.

The peers being the peers expect their peers to wait for them to catch on. Of course everybody has the birth right to wheel past at one's own speed. But what the peers expect least is being looked down upon by the smart buddy who is smarter than them for no fault of theirs. Besides, deep inside, everybody is aware of his/her own strength and weaknesses. So while waiting for others to complete their own run the most desirable thing to do is (i) to encourage the slow-paced ones and (ii) to discourage oneself about either blowing one's own trumpet or crying over spilt milk.

Waiting for the right opportunity to pay back a favour justifies one's company and proves one's worthiness.

Inspire

Friends are friends because they are the source of inspiration and strength that is much needed to excel in life.

The Capital 'I' in each of us is on the lookout for the compatible other's 'I', which would strengthen our individual confidence in our own capabilities and potentials.

Peers need careful handling to guard against jealousy, frustration and breach of trust.

❧

The ship of friendship needs dexterous manoeuvring to gain safe passage through rough weather, icebergs and also to avoid wreckage.

Though we all are aware of our own potentialities, there is always a fear of being looked down upon due to real as well as imaginary failures. Also there is a constant nagging thought about real and imaginary competitors. Besides, who knows what the near and dear ones would think of us if they found out what we are up to?

Arjuna, the great warrior suffered from the last-mentioned attitudinal disorder from which Sri Krishna had to rescue him in time by pumping in more than the required dose of inspirational and motivational talk. But for this timely inspirational Gita, the history of Mahabharat war could have been quite different.

Manoeuvre

The ship of friendship needs dexterous manoeuvring to gain safe passage through rough weather, icebergs and also to avoid wreckage.

The general misconception about friendship is that friends are forever and unlike any other serious relationship it does not need any special care and attention. Nothing in fact could be far from the truth.

From the traits of the Arjuna group the Sudama group and examples of Drona—Drupada pair, it is clear that like any love-based relationship, peer-based relationship also needs careful handling to guard against jealousy, frustration and breach of trust. A friendship gone sour is worse than a shipwreck as a lifelong source of malevolence gets created, which one does not know how to neutralize.

Besides, manoeuvring is required to protect or sustain any growing equation so that once firmly in place one can have faith in it without taking it for granted.

SINK

By now you must have guessed that once you WISH, ACT and decide to SWIM with your peers you can't disown and abandon them during difficult times. So you must be ready to SINK together too. And the acronym SINK stands for

S—Sacrifice

I—Incubate

N—Negotiate

K—Keep

Sacrifice

A sacrifice in time says a thousand things about the friend and the friendship.

Every relationship has to undergo the acid test at one time or the other. And at times to prove oneself, one has to be literally baptised by fire or sword or by anything else, which demands that the peer's interest be given priority. Such a show of selflessness in the matter of heart, emotion or money provides the stuff that the folklores are made up of.

NEGOTIATION

gives the

breathing space

and

time to work out

an

effective strategy.

It is almost like throwing oneself into floodwater to save a drowning non swimmer. The returns can't always be qualified and at times it might be a zero-sum game but to sink together means literally to sacrifice some or other self-interest and also to share the sufferings.

Incubate

Not only do premature babies need incubating but also does dexterity in peer management. At times a not-so-strong person experiences wavering of mind that strains the delicate threads of friendship. Many a relationship gets severed at such junctures creating a lifetime's regret and malevolence.

At such times, what actually is required is to give a long rope, extend a little more long hand, incubate the weaker peer against his/her failings and weaknesses, so that the friendship does not die a premature death.

Timely incubation allows the friendship to swim through a rough patch and re-entrench itself in a firm pedestal.

Negotiate

At the hour of need, the peers do bank upon the negotiating skills of those whom they trust.

It is a skill that everybody is not very cool about. Besides, it can't be entrusted to whosoever is willing or available to do it. Because everybody is not aware of our best interest. Especially in conflicting situations, when one is pitted

Keep
the doors and
windows open.
Allow the fresh
wind to come in
and stale air to go
out for ensuring a
healthy state of
affairs for the
peers.

against a powerful, deadly and malevolent adversary, negotiation is the best course of action that gives one the desired breathing space and time to work out an effective strategy. Of course, fight and flight are the two primary options available. However, both cause intentional or unintentional loss of resource and reputation, and hence are accepted as a last measure.

The peer who can mediate effectively and amiably without any hidden agenda of his/her own is cherished most by a person in need. This is what Krishna had proved time and again by doing the needful for his peers at the time of need.

Keeping the Arms Open

Keeping the doors and windows open to let the fresh wind come in and to let the stale air go out ensures a healthy state of affairs for the peers.

Any effective peer manager worth his/her training, skill and intuition knows it in the bones not only to welcome the peers with open arms but also to keep the inlets and outlets of heart, mind, thought and action open to change. It means sustaining the old attachments while encouraging the new alignments as well as braving troublesome and soured relationships. It also means keeping cool at the height of provocation. It also indicates keeping one's pace and time with the peers.

In a nutshell, it stands for keeping the spirit high and taking things sportively without losing sight of the crux of the matter. Alternatively it tells one to eat the apple and have it too.

This also keeps the ship of friendship afloat atop any headstrong iceberg.

MALEVOLENT PEERS (THE FOES/ENEMIES)

In our world of existence, where relationships are defined with referral points of malevolence and benevolence, the word "foe" points at every being that harbours malevolence—be it explicit, intrinsic, permanent, temporary, occasional or recurring. Of course, the Oxford dictionary defines the word "foe" simply as the enemy. The word "enemy" in its own turn is defined as a person who hates and who acts or speaks against a subject or against any other person. And "hate" stands for a feeling of dislike that could be strong or weak.

So, a "foe" is a person or a group of persons, hostile and inimical in attitude towards us or somebody else in "my/our camp", who try to act or speak in such a manner that it is not up to our liking at the least and is harmful to our interest. Hence, to begin with, we can safely say that a foe is a peer whom we have a reason to dislike and who certainly is not our well-wisher. Logically, this group of people fit into the "other or their camp", whereas the benevolent peers fit into "my or our camp".

THE OTHER CAMP

Since the "other camp" harbours the enemy, the general feeling or attitude that keeps our line of sight focused on them is a combination of suspicion, distrust and survival instinct. And as we discussed earlier, until and unless there is some osmosis of positive feelings through the windows of heart or economics, it is extremely difficult to compromise on these points. We have seen this in the life of both Guru Drona and his disciple Arjuna.

In fact, during infancy, the other camp is not that terrifying psychologically, as memory is not yet very stable to trouble anyone. Besides, the sportive spirit and the innocence of childhood make one forget and forgive quickly as complex socio-economic and egoistic interpersonal intricacies are yet to spread their wings.

MALEVOLENT PEERS

are persons

hostile and inimical

in attitude

who are

harmful to our

interests.

The dividing line starts when one enters the teens. The foes may be family foes, or community foes, or study group foes. In fact, childhood experiences with the foes have such a drastic impact on one that it leaves telltale signs of one's brush with destiny and influences one's approach towards life in a very definite manner.

The worst foes are those whom one encounters at the workplace and also who are competitors in matters of the heart. In other words, socio-economic and emotional foes are the foes from whom one expects and encounters the maximum hostility. They are the core group of the other camp, and at times are referred to as "hard core". Now, let us understand the most important aspect of this part of the book, i.e., why foes are foes.

WHY FOES ARE FOES

The very definition and explanation of the word **foe** indicates what exactly it stands for. Yet it is very essential to pinpoint the reasons, which fall into three broad categories

1.   Clash

2.   Bash

3.   Trash

In fact, a careful examination of our preceding discussion gives some indication of these three categories of broad reasons that justify our inherent dislike towards our foes. Let us study each of them separately for a better understanding:

Clash

The Oxford dictionary defines the word "clash" in seven different ways while taking it as a noun and explains it in six different ways when understood as a verb.

The noun form of clash is defined as follows:

❀	Fight	A short fight between two groups of people.
❀	Argument	An argument between two groups of people, who have different beliefs and ideas (a head-on clash between two leaders).
❀	Difference	The difference that exists between two different things/beings that are opposed to each other (a personality clash with somebody superior).
❀	Of two	A clash in the timetable/schedule of events.
❀	Of colours	The situation when two colours, designs, etc. look ugly when they are put together.

❀ Loud noise	Loud noise made by two metal objects being hit together (a clash of cymbals/swords).
❀ In sports	An occasion when two teams play against each other.

The verb form means the following:

❀ Fight	to compete in a contest.
❀ Argue	to disagree seriously in public.
❀ Be different	in beliefs, ideas or personalities.
❀ of two events	to happen simultaneously so that one goes unattended.
❀ of colours	of colours, styles or patterns that look ugly when put together.
❀ make loud noise	to hit together and make a noise.

From the above exhaustive explanations of the word, we can extract the crux and can make our own sub-headings under three categories, i.e., (i) clash of personality (ii) clash of interest (iii) clash of ideology.

Clash of personality

The personality is a complex combination of socio-economic background, grooming, attitude, education, looks, ambitions and approach towards life in general and events as well as beings in particular. There are charismatic persons, egotistic persons, flamboyant persons, reticent persons, arrogant persons, suspicious persons, naive persons and simpletons. We can go on and on to enlist the different types of personalities.

But what we must understand here is that it is the personality through which an individual is perceived and recognized by the others. Hence, two different personalities perceive each other in a very different manner, and the survival instinct goads them to take a stand different from each other. This causes clashes of personality on various issues, and acts as a breeding ground of enimity or hostility. The peer group adds fuel to this fire of difference, aggravating the differences further.

Clash of interest

Each one of us has certain basic and secondary needs, desires, wishes, ambitions and secret dreams and so do the others. While we are very protective about our needs and interests, there always is a lurking suspicion about that of the others. Given the limited space, time and resources that are available to us to achieve our goals and objectives, the mutual suspicion makes us wary of the other camp. And the other camp being human beings like us feel the same way, which results, in mutual dislikes and conflicts.

Besides, certain emotional factors like patriotism, regionalism, casteism, and communal feelings, cause clash of interests wherein one camp tries to discredit and look down upon the other camp.

Clash of ideology

It is derived from the root word 'idea' which stands for a belief or an impression in the mind about things and beings. The term ideology stands for a particular set of beliefs, which could be about economic, political, social, spiritual, scientific or interpersonal system and dynamics, especially held by a particular individual or a group. It in turn influences their behaviour towards self, and others. In fact, human beings are governed by two predominant factors, namely, habits and beliefs. Habits gradually turn into addictions. And when habits become die-hards, they result in clashes with others who are not like-minded people. Similarly, beliefs give rise to different sets of do's and don'ts. As a result, we get four different categories of people: (i) fanatic/dogmatists, (ii) liberals, (iii) autocrats, and (iv) democrats.

Fanatic/dogmatic people They are totally intolerant of the unlike-minded people. For them, life either has to be black or white, grey or colours are blasphemous. They believe in totally eliminating the "unlike" others so that their own supremacy can rule the roost and bring in a sense of harmony and security. For them, fanatic intolerance, superstition, and blind belief form the foundation of the struggle for power and prosperity. The factors of survival become a matter of premium.

Liberals They are those fluid-accommodative idealists who believe in variety and co-existence. They are the champions of the middle path and strive hard to bring in changes through due process of persuasion, conciliation and consensus. These are the people with whom the fanatics/ dogmatic people have a head-on clash. And this is the group, which at times falls apart when under intense and fatal attack from the fanatics, for want of strong team spirit and will power. Human history is full of examples of liberals being weathered away under the ruthless onslaught from dogmatists.

Autocrats Goaded by a sense of superiority complex and driven by the belief that the others are incompetent, useless, harmful and lesser mortals, the autocrats think of themselves as the change agents who do not hesitate to use force in order to get things done in a particular manner that they think is the ideal and the right way of doing things.

Democrats Democrats are those cousins of the liberals who believe in acting as per majority opinion. They believe in herd mentality and mediocrity, which carefully avoids extremities and novel experimentation until and unless it has the sanction of a large group of people, or society.

Democrats are poles apart from the autocrats and fanatics. So, there is an obvious chance of mutual dislike and clash. Mostly the political arena is their chosen place of existence and growth.

Bash

The dictionary meaning of "bash" is to hit very hard. And that of "bashing" are (i) very strong criticism of a person or group (ii) a series of physical attacks on a person or a group.

Now let us take a cue from the life of Sri Krishna. One of his die-hard foes was his own maternal uncle, Kamsa, who ruled from his capital Mathura. Anti-incumbency feelings had created such antipathy towards him that intelligentsia had started floating rumours about the advent of a future saviour who would be born to one of his cousins Devaki. As a result, he wanted to kill the lady, however good counsel prevailed and the lady and her spouse Vasudeva were kept under house arrest. All their six progenies were killed. However, the desperate couple with the help of their well-wishers manoeuvred the premature birth of the seventh child, found the surrogate mother for complete term, and deceived Kamsa by saying that the foetus got aborted. The child grew up to become Sri Krishna's elder brother Balarama.

Sri Krishna, the eighth child, was supposed to be the saviour of the masses and the terminator of Kamsa. Therefore, his parents immediately after his birth exchanged him with the daughter of Nanda, the chieftain of a nearby village across Yamuna.

Eventually Kamsa came to know about the deception, killed the girl child and pressed his secret agents into the mission of terminating his child foe. However, Sri Krishna survived all the attempts and lived up to the expectations and enacted the role that was so meticulously carved out for him by the intelligentsia and the soothsayers.

Though he was successful at getting even with Kamsa, Jarasandha (the latter's father-in-law) took up the cudgel on behalf of his widowed daughters and continued the bashing of Krishna and the Yadava class. The series of attacks by Jarasandha and his allies like Kalayavana were so severe that Sri Krishna was compelled to migrate along with his clan towards the west and settled in a far away place on the western coast called Dwaraka, an island off Gujarat coast.

In our own life, at times, we also become victims and find ourselves at the receiving end of wrath, attack and severe criticism for known and unknown reasons. Our own survival instinct too goads us to react in a befitting manner depending upon time, space, and mutual strength and weaknesses.

Thus the foes become foes because of bashing which could be verbal, physical, political, economic and societal or of any other form.

Trash

The dictionary meaning of trash varies from throw away/ unwanted things to an offensive word used for people or things one does not respect. In the context of our discussion all the meanings make sense. The foes are foes because they consider us as unwanted beings, who have nothing but nuisance value, and hence need to be weeded out or destroyed. And we all share the same feelings towards our foes.

The fundamental equation between foes being a negative one, it is logical to conclude that, at any given opportunity, both the opposing parties would try to destroy each other, malign each other and demean each other. The guiding principle behind all these is mutual malevolence and underestimation.

In fact, many a time this underestimation is so severe and detrimental that it leads to a crushing defeat on subsequent occasions. Here I am reminded of a story again from Sri Krishna's life.

After Kamsa's death, his father-in-law Jarasandha—the king of Magadha (present Bihar State of India)—swore to destroy Sri Krishna along with the Yadava republic clan. His mercenaries resorted to guerrilla attack initially to gauge the strength. Meanwhile Jarasandha sought alliance with Kalayavan, the ruler of western frontiers to plan a joint attack on Sri Krishna. To break this alliance and as a prelude to gauge the strength of his collective foes, Sri Krishna sent a diplomatic messenger. The messenger, so sent by him to Kalayavan, carried a box that contained a vicious cobra. The response and the return message came from Kalayavan in the form of an agile eagle wrapped inside a weatherproof bejewelled container.

Though the Yadavas could not exactly assess the foe's ally's strength, Sri Krishna simply pondered a while and asked his kith and kin to be ready for mass migration towards west coast where a new settlement would be organized. Further he cautioned them to manage the activities with utmost secrecy. This surprised all and sundry, as Sri Krishna was a fearless and brave warrior, and their saviour. Did it mean he had developed cold feet and was asking them to take to flight just out of cowardice? It was a harsh question that he had to answer.

Sri Krishna after pacifying his kinsmen, who were upset with the idea of mass migration told them that it was not wise to underestimate a foe. The symbolic message that Kalayavan had sent, i.e., the eagle, spoke of his superior aviation force vis-a-vis the infantry strength of the Yadavas. Besides the equation between the cobra and the eagle was that of food and predator. Though the cobra contains the life-taking poison, the eagle has the digestive power to have a meal of a cobra. So it is not wise to clash head-on with such an enemy. Instead, it is better to use the available time by planning camouflage and lying low. This would also give time to consolidate and strengthen all the armed wings of the Yadava clan.

What happened thereafter will be discussed in subsequent pages. But from the above incident, two lessons are very clearly described by Sri Krishna.

Never underestimate your foe.

When your foe belittles you, first try to find out the cause and then strengthen your own fort. Be aware of the fact that belittling the foe not only makes them show off their superiority but also unconsciously exposes their strengths and weaknesses.

i. Never underestimate your foe which may prove suicidal and

ii. If the foe is belittling you, first try to find out the cause and then strengthen your own fort.

In short, trashing the foe means (i) to malign and (ii) to belittle.

Maligning is a war of words with which the image of the foe and the morale of his team are expected to be targeted.

In response to belittling, the enemy not only outshows his/her own arrogance and shows off superiority but also unconsciously exposes his/her own strength and weaknesses. Thus, by arousing anger and other basic instincts in the enemy, which may blind their cool, calculative and rational decision, we can use the situation for our own benefit.

TYPES OF FOES

So far, we have learnt why foes are foes. However, it is necessary for us to know the types of foes. Because foes come in various grades and shades, proper management of the eventuality that one is likely to face due to their endeavours requires proper input about their general and specific characteristics, their abilities and weaknesses and one's own manoeuvrability for survival and success.

From the life history of our role model, Sri Krishna, we have gained some knowledge about his allies and enemies. Further, to classify the foes and to have a better understanding of the tools of malevolent-peer management, let us put them under following groups:

1. Kamsa group

2. Jarasandha group

3. Kalayavana group

4. Sishupala group

5. Duryodhana group

THE KAMSA GROUP

Kamsa, the king of Mathura, was the ruler of Yadava Republics. He forcefully acquired the crown by usurpation, after he came to know that he was an illegitimate child to his father Ugrasena. Ugrasena was the real king of the Yadavas. His wife was duped by an imposter (who was not a Yadav but belonged to another clan called the Rakshasas/Asuras) while she was on a tour. As a result of that sexual encounter, she gave birth to Kamsa. Since no one knew the truth about his paternity he enjoyed the privileges of a crown prince and also acquired strong military alliances through his marriage and other viable means.

The disclosure of the secret behind his birth by his foes at a very strategic time took him by surprise. Feeling insecure about his own future, Kamsa placed his foster father Ugrasena under house arrest and ascended the throne. He had the total support of all his allies including that of his father-in-law Jarasandha, the mighty ruler of Magadha (present Bihar). Ever since his usurpation of throne, the influential coteries of the Yadava clan and the intelligentsia had harboured negative feelings towards him for the two most important and obvious reasons (i) his biological illegitimacy and (ii) his illegal means of acquiring the crown.

The Yadavas had adopted republican monarchy. And such outright imposition of kingship on them had hurt their feelings. Though by applying various art and craft of statecraft and administration, Kamsa must have tried to win them over, yet he was not completely successful. As a result, anti-incumbency feelings were whipped by the supporters of the other camp through every available means. The soothsayers and the fortune-tellers played a big role in moulding the public opinion.

Though he could sail through these obstacles by means of Sama (counselling), Dana (bribe/monetary gratification), Danda (punishment/fear of punishment) and Bheda (diplomacy/divide and rule), somehow and somewhere the weakest link gave way. Let us learn the personality traits of this group of people before we analyse how these people are/were handled by their friends and foes and vice versa.

Personality Traits of Kamsa Group

The dominant and recessive traits of Kamsa group of people are as follows:

- They are brave and bold, and hence they don't hesitate to call a spade a spade.
- They are susceptible to extreme likes and dislikes.
- They have strong affiliation for power.
- They believe in the supremacy of authority and statecraft.
- They are good at mustering strong and superior allies.
- They are poor in seeing through deceit and double talk.

❀ They have a harsh exterior with an emotional and insecure inner self.

❀ They exhibit poor understanding of individual as well as mass psychology.

❀ They are prone to coterie politics.

❀ They cultivate a brash, harsh and arrogant public image of themselves.

❀ They believe in the Machiavellian principle, i.e., the prince should be more feared than loved.

❀ They are good military and authoritative leaders, who inspire amongst the allies trust but somehow lose out in the department of mass followers.

❀ They are good at wresting and sustaining power but are poor at feeling the mass pulse.

❀ As allies they are dependable and as foes they need watchful surveillance.

❀ They are capable of changing tactics but poor at bidding for time.

❀ They are very poor at keeping their agenda hidden.

❀ They need to depend upon a reliable strategist.

❀ They know what they want out of their lives and don't hesitate to pay any price to reach the goal.

❀ For them, end justifies the means.

KAMSA GROUP

* Inner insecurity

* Egocentric

* Dependable allies

* Observable foes

* Power hungry

* Crafty and cruel

They are the easiest group to handle because of their obvious strengths and weaknesses.

Among the malevolent peers, the Kamsa group is the easiest group to handle because of their obvious strength and weaknesses. One has to keep them at a safe distance, lest one may find them occupying one's own chair. They are capable of backstabbing, as they are power hungry and egocentric. Their alliances are based on mutual empathy, as they understand each other's inner insecurity pretty well.

JARASANDHA GROUP

Jarasandha, who lends his name to this generic group, had a very interesting initiation to life. In the great epic Mahabharata, it is said that he was born with so much of physical deformities that his parents—the king and queen of Magadha (present Bihar state)—had abandoned him. A witch named Jara, by her extraordinary surgical means, rectified the biological deformities and restored the child to his parents. The repentant and grateful parents named the child after the witchdoctor and hence the name Jarasandha. The favour of this foster mother blessed the young prince with extraordinary strength of body and mind. In course of time, he ascended the throne and became a very powerful king in the true sense of the term. Keeping with the tradition of the time, he gained political and military alliances through each and every available means including that of matrimony.

His daughters were married to Kamsa, the then ruler of Yadavas. In terms of political and military strength as well as legitimacy, Jarasandha was more powerful than Kamsa.

The enmity between Kamsa and Krishna made Jarasandha a natural foe/enemy of Krishna. In fact, the Yadavas were no match for Jarasandha's superior military tactics, alliances and strategy. The guerilla attack, combined with the invasion in collusion with Yavanas, had forced Sri Krishna and the Yadavas to migrate to the west coast deserting the city of Mathura. Unable to defeat him in an open battle, Sri Krishna had to get him killed at the hands of Bhima, an elder brother of Arjuna in a duel of wrestling, that too after entering Jarasandha's capital in the guise of Brahmins.

Personality Traits of Jarasandha Group

The characteristic traits of this group of people are as follows:

- ❀ They are determination and courage personified.

- ❀ They are the survivors and the victors even in most odd situations.

- ❀ They are excellent managers and strategists and can give their enemies good run for their worth.

- ❀ Brave and bold, they seek equivalent allies to further their interest.

- ❀ Steadfast in protecting and living up to the expectations of their kith, kin and allies.

- ❀ They are good leaders in their own way and are the most formidable foes.

❀ Thorough in their field, they are fiercely competitive and proud.

❀ They are good managers of change and resources.

❀ They exhibit patience and foresight.

❀ Pragmatic and practical, they compel time and tide to keep pace with them.

❀ They never mind changing tactics and updating technology.

❀ They are ruled only by the head and objectives.

The Jarasandha group is the most formidable amongst the foe groups, and due to their inherent strength and physical proximity they remain a source of constant threat. Since their existence can't simply be wished away, managing this group of foes needs the most versatile management skills. Being good at both change-management and change-resistance they are to be taken seriously if one intends to survive and counter their menace. We will learn how to do it in a later section.

KALAYAVANA GROUP

According to the author of the epic Mahabharata, Kalayavana was the ruler of Yavanas (most probably of hilly tribes of western frontiers of India or that of the area adjacent to Persia and who were black or dark by complexion).

JARASANDHA GROUP

* Courage personified

* Excellent strategists

* Pragmatic and practical

* Determined

They are the most formidable foes.

Like Jarasandha and Kamsa he also had an interesting background of being born under strange circumstances. It so happened that once a sage paid a visit to the royal court of Yadavas for some work. Due to severe penance and austerities, he was not only emaciated but also had lost his potency. His shrunk genitals became a source of mirth for the young and arrogant prince. Humiliated and annoyed the sage vowed to get even. To fulfil his vow he started self medication using certain ingredients that contained iron.

On regaining potency he looked for a woman who could bear him a child as a surrogate. With much difficulty he found one Gopi (cowherdess) who successfully delivered a male progeny for him in exchange of some blessing. Thereafter the sage arranged for adoption and the child was brought up by the childless Yavana king who was assured by the sage that the child would grow up to vanquish the Yadava republics. It is the same child who became renowned as Kalayavana and became a sworn enemy of the Yadava clan.

Like Krishna who was groomed from childhood to rebel against his uncle and Yadava ruler Kamsa, Kalayavana was trained and motivated to project himself as the destroyer of the Yadavas.

Eventually on invitation from Jarasandha, Kalayavana attacked Mathura, first adopting guerilla warfare, later challenging Krishna and Yadavas in open confrontation.

The attacks were so vicious that Krishna had no other option but to advise mass emigration to the west coast (Dwaraka). Finally, Kalayavana was burnt to death in a cave by a strange strategy executed by Krishna, as he could not otherwise be defeated in open warfare.

Personality Traits of Kalayavana Group

The characteristic traits of Kalayavana group of people are as follows:

- They are born leaders.

- They are goal-oriented and ruthless.

- Very intelligent, they are a deadly combination of brain and brawn.

- Technologically superior, they somehow fall prey to cunning strategies.

- They inspire confidence as well as loyalty among friends.

- Among foes they prefer to be feared.

- Committed to their goals however they somehow fail to see through deceit.

- Brave and bold they are power-personified.

- Emotions and love do not make any sense to them but they have full understanding of revenge.

KALAYAVANA GROUP

* Power personified

* Intelligent

* Extremists

* Goal-oriented

They are the deadliest and the most difficult-to-manage foes.

▓   They are extremists who believe in destroying the enemy in totality.

▓   Selective in choosing their friends and foes.

▓   They are very successful in sustaining power and leadership.

Among the foes the Kalayavana group is the deadliest and is the most difficult to manage. One needs to pull strength, technology as well as strategies together with due application of mind if one wants to survive their threat. Apart from being brave and bold one needs to be dexterous in psychology and principles of mental warfare to counter the influence of this group.

SHISHUPALA GROUP

Shishupala was one of the paternal cousins of Krishna. Ruler of the Chedi kingdom, he was a competitor of Krishna not only in political leadership but also in matrimonial alliances. Inimical towards Krishna since childhood, he survived Krishna's malevolence because of the latter's promise to Shishupala's mother to forgive one hundred misdemeanours on his part.

Their enmity had increased manyfold after Krishna kidnapped princess Rukmini and married her against the wishes of her father and brother, who had fixed her marriage with Shishupala. This grouse manifested itself in an outburst of abuses against Krishna during Rajasuya Yaga of Yudhishtra, the eldest brother of Arjuna. Sri Krishna used his unique weapon Sudarshana Chakra and decapitated Shishupala in the presence of assembled kings and settled the matter once for all.

Personality Traits of Shishupala Group

The characteristic traits of Shishupala group of people are:

- They are haughty and proud.
- They lack strategy and foresight.
- Though leaders of middle stature, they always aspire for supremacy.
- Rigid and arrogant, they don't pay much attention towards finer aspects of managing friends and foes.
- Inflexible in their attitude, they fail to acquire right friends at the right time or place.
- Envy and pride personified, they are prone to taking the wrong side which costs them dearly.
- Lack of innovation makes them lag behind in technology and management skills.
- Though committed towards friends and allies they are neither emotional nor loving.
- Though always aspiring for excellence, they somehow fail to scale the dizzy heights.

SHISHUPALA GROUP

* **Pride personified**

* **Inflexible attitude**

* **Lack of skills**

* **Lack foresight**

They are the weakest and the most vulnerable foes.

⚜ They never command mass following and admiration.

⚜ They never know what gratitude means.

Among the foes Shishupal a group is the weakest and the most vulnerable one. They are easier to manage because of their inherent weaknesses. But one can't take them for granted, as they always remain a source of irritation and embarrassment. Lack of cunning makes them the plainest among the foes. They always blow hot, and hence are very predictable in their behaviour and action. Though they have the capacity to be the winners, they end up as losers sinking their own boat due to wrong choices and short-sighted management policies. They are the permanent foes.

DURYODHANA GROUP

Duryodhana as such was not the sworn enemy of Krishna but was a circumstantial enemy as he always went along with the other camp. Though like Pandavas he and his hundred brothers were cousins of Krishna, the family feud about succession to the throne of Hastinapura—the capital of the Kauravas/Pandavas—pitted him against Arjuna group. So Arjuna's foe became Krishna's foe.

Besides, Duryodhana, the eldest of Dhritarastra's children, was a staunch supporter of Shishupala a sworn enemy of Krishna and formed alliance with Karna, the abandoned premarital child of Pandavas' mother Kunti.

Karna was a sworn enemy and competitor of Arjuna not only as a warrior but also as a contender for the hand of Draupadi. This placed him in the other camp.

Finally prior to the commencement of the Mahabharata war when both he and Arjuna went to Sri Krishna seeking his support, by opting for Sri Krishna's army he naturally became the other side leaving the field open to Arjuna to avail the benefits of Sri Krishna's friendship and management skills. This made him the circumstantial foe of Krishna.

Personality Traits of Duryodhana Group

The characteristic traits of Duryodhana group are as follows:

- Proud and arrogant, they are over-ambitious.

- Absolutely goal-oriented, they believe in adopting means that fructify their goals.

- Shrewd and confident they are trendsetters in making new friends.

- Leaders in their own right they are good at commanding loyalty from their own camp people.

- Wise and cunning they know that (but for some sworn enemies) in life there are no permanent friends and no permanent foes.

- Versatile and talented, they excel in their chosen field and know how to eliminate competitors.

▧ While managing friends and foes, they use force, technology and strategy all in required combination to optimize their gain.

▧ They are dubious and can offer lip service to deceive their enemies.

▧ Poor negotiators they can cause and manage proxy war very well.

▧ Don't believe in peaceful co-existence with the other camp.

▧ They are firm believers in zero-sum game.

▧ It is not possible for them to forget and forgive any insult or injury.

▧ For them the enemies' enemy is the dearest friend. However they don't mind applying divide and rule policy and win over enemies' friends also.

▧ Least emotional they believe in real politics and further their socio-economic interest very zealously.

Among the foes, the Duryodhana group is the most sophisticated and dicy one to handle. Though they don't affect one's interest directly their enmity with the people of one's own camp leaves one with the least choice. They force or persuade people to take sides and exhibit explicit proof of loyalty or disloyalty. Their ambition and greed results in total destruction. To manage them, one has

DURYODHANA GROUP

* Wise

* Cunning

* Proud and arrogant

* Dubious

* Least emotional

They are the most sophisticated and dicy ones to handle.

to see through their superior mental games and outmanoeuvre them.

MANAGEMENT TOOLS OF KRISHNA

The foes are threats to one's life, inheritance, assets, support systems and prosperity. So, let us now learn how to manage them. Before that let us know the methods that were used by Sri Krishna in handling these people.

SELF-MANAGEMENT

Apart from sense of humour and self-confidence, what helped Sri Krishna in managing himself vis-a-vis his foes was his acute sense of timing the events, organizational skills, deep understanding of his own strength and weaknesses, foresight and love, and above all was the cleverly executed strategy. An excellent understanding of human psychology and behavioural models helped him to project his own influence in a very amiable and balancing manner. Pragmatic and intrinsic understanding of his own limitations and the strength of others, kept his own ego and goals under due check. Since childhood, he fought his own battles, and hence, sifted both his brain and brawn as per his own judgement. This helped him in rising above the peer pressure.

His prudence had goaded him to restore the crown to the seniormost Yadava, Ugrasena, after the death of Kamsa.

He followed the same pattern in the case of Shishupala and Jarasandha, where he enthroned their progeny/heir instead of appropriating the prize to himself. This earned him goodwill in the other camp.

Surprisingly, he never went out of his way to cultivate allies or neutralize the foes. While sustaining natural friends, he concentrated on upgrading and improving upon his own skills, technologies and expertise. As far as foes are concerned, he believed in giving them as well as himself a long rope before pulling the strings.

The discus or the Sudarshana Chakra symbolized his military superiority, self-control as well as fight-to-finish attitude while managing the foes. Pushed to the corner, he believed in asserting his might without any emotional wobbling. While buying time in tricky situations, he never underestimated his enemies and exhibited infinite patience before delivering the decisive blow. In fact, he was much annoyed with Shishupala, because he had an eye on his Sudarshana Chakra. It is a unique characteristic trait of his self-management that he did not mind gifting his flute to Radha, but he never ever allowed anyone else to operate his discus (Sudarshana Chakra).

Besides satiating his own desires and will, he did draw the line for himself very pragmatically. This was exhibited by kidnapping Rukmini against the wishes of Shishupala and her kith and kin; yet at the same time refusing to contest for the hand of Draupadi. Nobody else in his place could have taken such a decision. All his marital alliances were guided by the decisions of his heart. All his friendships were based upon selfless goodwill and his enmity was a matter of fact. Unlike many of his contemporaries, he kept out of marital alliances with political overtones.

MANAGING KAMSA GROUP

Though ambitious and cunning, the Kamsa group people carry the burden of a very low self-esteem. Due to certain past experiences, they feel very insecure and paranoid by imaginary threats and competitors. This inner insecurity and low self-esteem is exploited by their adversaries as well as the coterie to the fullest possible extent in waging psychological warfare.

Sri Krishna had to abort many an attempt on his life, which was all planned by the coterie of Kamsa. However, the parental support, the support and wishes of the kith and kin, and the extended family saw him through these ordeals. Otherwise he and his elder brother Balarama could have died at the hands of Kamsa immediately after their birth.

In order to escape the enemy's wrath, Krishna had to spend his childhood incognito at his foster parents' place, which adversely affected his education and natural growth as a child. In managing this foe, Krishna depended upon proxy and psychological warfare waged by his protectors and elders, till such time he came of age. Once physically strong and mature, the confrontation was managed openly by defying Kamsa.

Here, the management principle is the complete routing and elimination of the foe so that the matter was settled once for all.

MANAGING JARASANDHA GROUP

Being a friend of the primary enemy by virtue of marital alliances, (going by the logic that makes the enemies' friend a severe enemy), this enemy group affects one's interest severely.

Initially, he managed this enemy/foe by available counter measures and thereafter he retreated and bought time to reorganize his strategies. This also gave him and the people of his camp the much-needed breathing space and some sort of stability, because under the onslaught of enemy pressure, the Yadavas had started cracking up. Only after stabilizing at a new place and securing the active support of the Arjuna group (Pandava brothers) that he could work out the strategy of deceit and cunning whereby Bhima's (the second elder brother of Arjuna) expertise in wrestling and boxing was utilized effectively to eliminate Jarasandha.

Here, the crux of the matter is that a synergy of brawn and weapon was initially not enough to counter this foe's strength. So, alternative strategies had to be adopted after feigning a lie low phase.

MANAGING KALAYAVANA GROUP

Kalayavana was a born and indoctrinated enemy with a mission to destroy not only the opposition leader, i.e., Sri Krishna, but also had the surcharged vision of a mass elimination of the other camp.

This was the worst ever combination that one could have in a foe. When Jarasandha was trying to protect his daughters' right by avenging the death of his son-in-law, Kalayavana was trying to settle a score and uphold his biological father's honour. In other words, while Jarasandha was trying to avenge the injury (fatal), Kalayavana was out there to make the other camp pay greatly for an insult. This emotional surcharge not only made Kalayavana deadlier, but it also made him vulnerable, because as an emotionally charged man, he could not have the required coolness to see through the other camp's deceit.

Krishna managed him initially by judging his wit and foresight (we have already learnt about the diplomatic war) and thereafter by working out a flight and finally misleading him to a death trap in the cave.

The severity of conviction among this group of people makes them the fanatics, which is intelligently manipulated by the Krishna group by show of dexterous flexibility and variety of strategy.

MANAGING SHISHUPALA GROUP

The haughty and foolhardiness of Shishupala left Sri Krishna with two options. One was to take pity and forgive as long as it was tolerable, and the second was the simple elimination. In fact, Shishupala was no match for Sri Krishna. Being goaded by pride and overambitiousness, he always tried to prove himself superior. Though a born prince and a king, his lack of maturity and foresight made him a pawn in the hands of people like Duryodhana who incited his haughtiness to embarrass Sri Krishna in public life. Though none of them was held responsible for the act of abetment and incitement, it was Shishupala who bore the brunt.

Sri Krishna had adopted the principles of tolerance and forgiveness vis-à-vis Shishupala. The moment things went beyond his tolerance limit the bubble burst. Thereafter without wasting any time on any kind of debate or wavering of mind, instant decision was taken and the discus (Chakra) was authorized to execute it. The result was the total elimination of the source of nuisance for all times to come.

From this, the lesson is that each of us should respect the virtue of tolerance and forgiveness in a foe and should not take it for granted. And to drive the message home one should not hesitate as and when harsh decisions are required to be taken.

MANAGING DURYODHANA GROUP

Being a camouflaged and situational foe, Sri Krishna kept Duryodhana and his brothers at arms length though his elder brother, Balarama, had favourable feelings towards him. In fact to make an ally out of Balarama, Duryodhana learned the higher nuances of mace-fight from him. This learning not only made his skills at par with that of Bhima's but also won the heart of Balarama. For that reason, Balarama refused to take the side against his disciple during Mahabharata war and absented himself on the pretext of spiritual tourism (teertha yatra).

This made Krishna's task easier. Free from fraternal pressure, he could support whole-heartedly Arjuna's cause though much before the war of Mahabharat, his alliance with Arjuna and Draupadi group was a well-known thing. Though he did no harm to Duryodhana as such, neither did Duryodhana to him, yet the proxy war had put them in two different camps. Due to his commitment towards Arjuna and Draupadi groups, he refused to change the camp and used all his might, and military skills, as well as cunning (intellectually) against the Duryodhana group to earn victory for Arjuna and Draupadi.

The defeat of Duryodhana group in the war of Mahabharata that spanned over eighteen bloody days was a foregone conclusion, though Krishna did assist Duryodhana by providing him military and logistic support

FOE-MANAGEMENT SLIDE-BAR

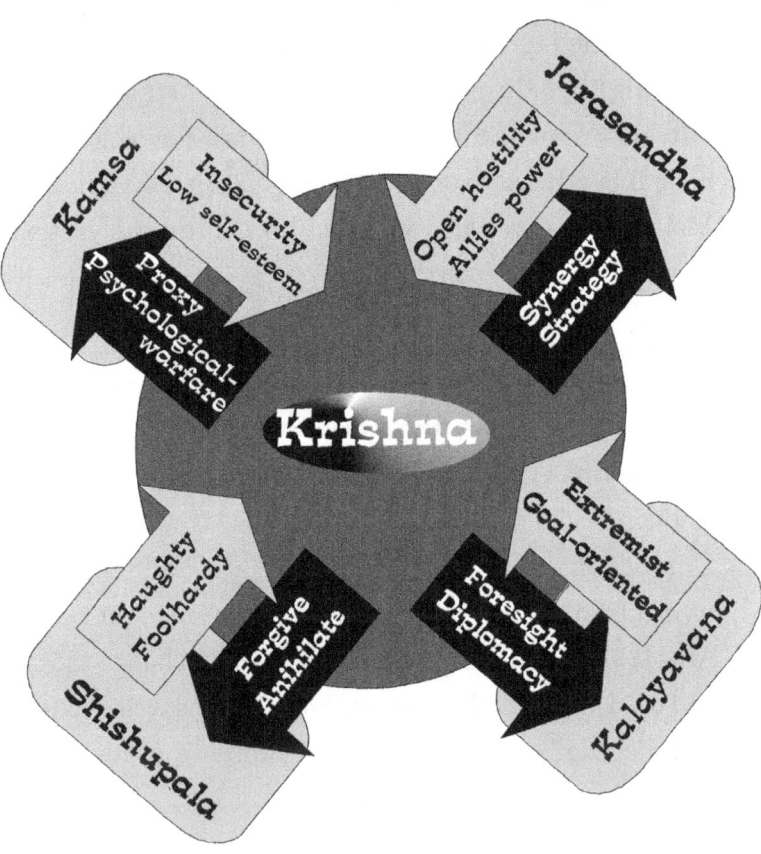

in terms of trained manpower and weaponry. While his army fought for Duryodhana, he stood by Arjuna and Draupadi to further their cause.

This is a very strange and difficult way of managing a foe. The strangeness is further strengthened by the fact that he had vowed not to use any weapon during this war. It meant that he had not appeared as an accomplished warrior, i.e., he never used his discus (the management tool) to eliminate the foe. But like a non-playing captain, he was manoeuvring the fatal process as per his will and wisdom.

Even for killing Duryodhana, he made use of Bhima's skills in mace fight and broke a few rules of the war to give that much required final push. Against the honoured rules of mace-war he instigated Bhima to hit Duryodhana below the waist and to break his thighs. Duryodhana died of grievous injury. Though by doing this, Sri Krishna was risking the displeasure of his elder brother Balarama, his commitment towards his benevolent peer and brother-in-law, Arjuna, got the upper hand.

By doing this, he justified the old saying, "All is fair in war and love".

MODERN MANAGEMENT SKILLS

To further articulate our understanding of the principle of foe-management, let us organize the core points of Krishna's hypotheses in our own management terms. These core

ALL IS FAIR IN
WAR AND LOVE.

points, for the convenience of understanding, are placed under five different groups with the acronyms: (i) FIGHT (ii) FLIGHT (iii) FEIGN (iv) FORGET. Let us take up each individually.

FIGHT

Since the foes are the foes due to clash of interest, ideology and personality, the basic objective in managing malevolent foes is to fight it out in whatever means one is comfortable with. The acronym FIGHT stands for

F—Fight

I—Instigate

G—Galvanize

H—Hit

T—Topple

Fight

Each one of us has to fight the malicious intentions and actions of our foes. Fight is a natural instinct of all living beings though the mode of execution and exhibition differs from person to person and species to species. The survival instinct and scarcity of resources make it a law of nature to ensure survival of the fittest. Since the human beings are at the top of the food chain and have no predators as such to limit their number, it is perhaps a trick of nature to make them fight amongst themselves.

Otherwise, given the uncertainty of lifespan, insecurity of childhood and old age, there is no reason why people like Kamsa should put their own as well as others' existence at stake on the basis of a mere prediction about some unforeseen future event.

The basic objective in a fight is to get even in terms of result to prove one's own superiority. It is a zero-sum game where one wins and the other loses. Though truce may be a third option, it is mostly seen and used as a method to buy time and breathing space for a renewed and decisive attack. So, willy-nilly one should always be ready for a fight, as this is the oldest and most effective mode of foe-management.

Instigation

Instigation is the oldest trick of challenging the foe.

Those who have watched WWF or any kind of martial art, know how a foe is aroused into blind fury by the opponent, because anger or fury is the worst enemy of a martial artist. An overdose of adrenalin always causes overdrive and overreaction prompting one either to flee or to fight that results in emotional as well as physical exhaustion. And once exhausted, it is easier to defeat the enemy.

This being a double-edged weapon however one should be wise enough to see through the tricks of an enemy. And while instigating the opponent, one should keep one's

F ight
I nstigate
G alvanize
H it
T opple

F lee
L eave
I nnocuous
G raft
H ide
T rouble

F eign
E scape
I ntermediary
G uard
N egotiate

F orgive
O bstruct
R emember
G ather
I gnore
V isualize
E ntangle

Modern Management Skills

own cool at any cost so as not to fall victim to the same trap.

Sri Krishna had applied this to all his enemies. In fact he had applied it not only to arouse anger and overdrive but also to instigate inertia and inaction. For example, he made Shikhandi (the princess of Kashi who had become a male after a sex-change operation) to fight against Bhisma, the great patriarch of the Duryodhana group, which made Bhisma give up his weapon. Further he made the Pandavas mention the news of the death of an elephant named Ashwathama and allowed the rumour to reach the ears of Drona, the preceptor who was fighting for Duroyodhana. Incidentally, Ashwathama was also the name of Acharya Drona's son and as anticipated by Krishna, Drona gave up fighting out of grief on hearing this. This made victory easier for the Arjuna group.

So, instigation is a strategy by which the enemy is made to respond in a predictable manner that suits one's own purpose to the detriment of the enemy's camp.

Galvanize

By galvanizing the followers as well as the foes into activities, the leaders achieve their individual as well as collective goals.

Nothing could be truer than this. The mere prediction about Sri Krishna's birth had sent his number-one enemy Kamsa into a whirlwind of scheming actions. Though

Sri Krishna's kith and kin were at the receiving end, but for this the history of Mahabharata and lifestory of Sri Krishna could have been different. Most probably he could not have emerged as a supreme leader of his time.

In fact, it is this capability to galvanize that causes the fear psychosis in the mind of the foes and in the other camp. Because while working as a positive motivator for the own camp, it also affects the priority, mobilization and motivation of the other camp where the person is regarded as the fountainhead of opposition.

It is a good technique of pro-active foe management for those who want to keep the enemies' attention engaged. It is like having a military exercise at the border to make the neighbouring country anxious, or it could be like a war of advertisement whereby one tries to compel the competitor either to improve or to perish.

Hit

The time-tested wisdom says that there is a time to hit and there is a time to retreat. Whether it is in politics or war, in business or sports, in any and every field of activity, competition is very essential to hit the target. Hitting the right target at the right time and at the right place makes the difference between a winner and a loser.

Of course, over the years, targets keep changing, as we have learnt from the life of Sri Krishna. However, the objective always remains the same, i.e., at times it was a matter of winning a battle, at times the hand of a princess was at stake, at some other time the day-to-day survival and at another time it was the honour of the self which needed attention.

The strength of a foe is adjudged from the capability of hitting the interest of the adversary in such a manner so as to cause losses to the other camp and bring gains to the own camp.

So the foe management principle here is to hit the foes interest both directly and indirectly whenever one gets an opportunity to ensure proper and timely deterence.

Topple

Since it is very rare to have a win-win situation between the foes, it is better to play the toppling game to safeguard one's own interest.

In general, an enmity between two opposite camps is based on mutual mistrust and suspicion whereby one party always perceives the other party to be engaged in the act of destabilization, subversion and abetment. The inner insecurity of losing out and getting defeated keeps one always worried and concerned.

The word **topple** means to make one lose the position of power and authority. It also means to make one unsteady before making one fall. In other words, it is both abetment

There is a time to hit and time to retreat.

Hitting the right target at the right time and the right place makes the difference between a winner and a loser.

and commission of the act. The enemy can be made emotionally and otherwise unsteady by adopting various methods of direct as well as indirect inimical activities, propaganda, etc. And once the target is unsteady, it is easier to topple.

The word of caution here is to watch out for the foe's planning and move on the same line for one's own protection.

FLIGHT

Under stress or face-to-face with challenge, the survival instinct exhibits two basic symptoms, i.e., fight and/or flight. Though in general the tendency is to eulogize fight and look down upon flight, reality bytes tell one to use both as per requirement and convenience. The acronym FLIGHT stands for

> F—Flee
>
> L—Leave
>
> I—Innocuous
>
> G—Graft
>
> H—Hide
>
> T—Trouble

Flee

Fleeing at the opportune time saves one of the disgraces of losing out.

There is a Sanskrit proverb,'*Jah palayate Sah jivate*'. It means that the one who flees in time survives. Of course, on face value, this sounds cowardice and unpalatable. But those who have/had the chance of fighting it out in any field of competition know how foolhardy it is to face extinction without giving oneself the chance to reorganize and re-strategize.

In fact, the word "flee" means to leave a person or place very quickly because of possible danger. Fleeing is synonymous with a period of convalescence or recuperation. In the battlefield, it can be downright escape both as a necessity as well as a strategy. In the market economy, it means lying low and observing the market trend before deciding any course of action. So, while managing the foes and malevolent peers, it is at times wise to flee so as to give space and time to observe as well as to plan, and is advisable to retaliate only when one is confident enough to wrest the victory.

Leave

In the subject of foe management, it is more of a rule than an exception to leave the victory to oneself.

In mathematics as well as in death, the word leave symbolizes remainder. Remainder means the leftovers, like sediments, which either enrich one's life or despoil one's crop for several seasons.

Watch out

for the

foes' planning

and

plan your move

to

safeguard

your interest.

In the context of peer management, it is the remainder of one's management skills, which either makes one leave the field for the other or compels the other to leave the fruit. Here "leaving" proves to be beneficial. However, at times, one is also compelled to actually leave the malevolent ones alone. It works like a double-edged sword by making the enemy believe in the wrong notion that one is either exhausted or defeated. It also makes the enemy wait and watch thereby testing his/her patience. And as far as self-interest is concerned, the objective always is to claim the victory, which is the remainder in any competition/conflict, for oneself.

Innocuous

Innocuous appearance and façade helps a lot in luring the foe into complacency. There are two different approaches of foe management—obvious, and innocuous. The obvious method makes no bones about one's intentions and feelings. The antagonism becomes apparent, visible and well known. Accordingly the strategies also become the subject of study for countermeasures.

However, prudence says that by making things too obvious one gives away too much. Known enemies become sworn enemies, which hardens the ego, thereby jeopardizing the chance of reconciliation. Hence, the intelligent ones prefer to adopt the other method.

By maintaining an innocuous appearance, one gains the benefit of doubt. The non-threatening appearance and attitude work like a trap for the unsuspecting enemy. It also gives one the space and time to scheme and execute one's victory.

Graft

Grafting one's own interest and befooling the foe speaks highly of one's capability of foe-management.

The cuckoo and the crow are never mutual friends. The former though endowed with a beautiful voice is a shrewd one that never troubles itself with the task of nurturing the progeny. Poor crow befooled by the feather colour and the dumb voice of the junior cuckoo labours hard to bring it up only to end-up disappointed. Nevertheless the cuckoo's interest gets furthered.

The traditional Indian wisdom speaks of Dana (bribe/ monetary gratification) and Bheda (infiltration/diplomacy), which collectively means the use of graft to gain inroads into an alien territory or the area of interest. Planting spies, compromising the honesty and integrity of enemies' aides and putting one's own trusted ones inside the enemies' garrison, helps a lot in breaking the enemies' strong hold. Once the internal secrets of the other camp are known, it is but a matter of time before one claims victory.

Hide

Once in a while, foe management should be taken as a sport, where one should play hide- and- seek to gauge the other camp's strength and weaknesses vis-a-vis that of one's own.

Hiding one's intentions as well as assets is a kind of strategy that one needs to master to have an upper hand.

In our present context, we know it is the flaunting of strength, arrogance and superiority that had seen the downfall of Kamsa and Shishupala. Contemporary history is full of examples of such cases. People like Napoleon and Hitler did not know how to rein in excessive exhibition of strength and power. As a result, groups of nations gathered against them and saw their downfall.

Our hero Sri Krishna had to go into hiding from day one till he attained the age to counter the threat. And even thereafter he had to evade the responsibility of the crown in order to avoid jealousy. Though a kingmaker and the supreme political/religious leader of his time, he never enthroned himself formally nor encouraged the growth of any organized religion around his philosophy.

Trouble

Troubleshooting is one of the most effective means of foe management. It has two different aspects. First, shooting the trouble caused by the enemy, and the second is causing the trouble for the enemy.

Gauge the

other camp's

strength

and

weaknesses

as well as

that of

one's own.

The idea itself means catching the bull by its horns while being careful about its kicks. In other words, it means meeting the trouble halfway as well as forcing the trouble-maker to come forward for a show of strength. This principle believes in the saying "offence is the best defense."

But one should be careful while applying it, as it may rebound on oneself if one is not properly prepared to handle the situation. Besides one should always work out some contingency plan to handle any unfavourable eventuality. The way Sri Krishna handled Jarasandha's downfall is the most relevant example of this principle.

FEIGN

Rampant amongst the animal kingdom, "FEIGN" is the catch-word when one wants to evade the attention of the enemies. The chameleon-like behaviour, which feigns by camouflage, is a very powerful survival tactic when one wants to avoid direct confrontation for one's own interest. In the instant case, the word FEIGN stands for

F—Feign

E—Escape

I—Intermediary

G—Guard

N—Negotiate

Catch
the bull
by its
horns
while being
careful
about
its
kicks.

Feign

Feigning innocence and ignorance at the right place saves one of inquiry, embarrassment as well as loss when pitted against a powerful foe (who could be known or unknown).

Feign or pretension is a very powerful tool of foe management, as it not only helps in hiding the true strength and intention but also distracts the enemies' attention. By pretending what one actually is not, one can create an ambience of complacency and inaction to lure the enemy into a trap. Besides it can also be used as a trick to lie low during unfavourable times. In the animal kingdom, animals change their body colour to pretend what they are not and thereby mingle with the surroundings and actually befool the predator. Some people think that this tool is meant for the meek and the weak, but wisdom tells us that it is equally useful for anybody who is in a trying situation.

Escape

When trapped, escaping should be the first priority before one plans a counterattack.

The word escape means getting away (physically) from a dangerous or an unpleasant situation or place. It also means forgetting the unpleasant or difficult for a short time. In the context of foe management both are applicable. Sri Krishna, as a child, had to escape from the dungeon from the very inception. And thereafter had to escape a number of fatal attempts on his life.

Feigning
or
pretension
is a very
powerful tool
of foe
management.

In fact, the word escapism has gathered much infamy as some people overuse it as an excuse for not doing certain things. But in foe management, it is a piece of practical wisdom to get away as soon as possible so as to minimize the damage.

Intermediary

The presence of an intermediary is always an asset in foe-management. Sri Krishna himself acted as an intermediary between the Kauravas and the Pandavas on several occasions. Not only in the political arena but also in ordinary day-to-day life, the intermediary plays an important role in either cementing or souring an equation. They are the catalysts who have the capacities either to trigger a phase of conciliation and good rapport or to drag the things to the point of no return. Either way their importance can't be ignored.

Both in war and in peace, the presence of a benevolent intermediary is a must because it works as an agent to protect the interest of the involved parties. True to the meaning of the word the intermediaries help the other people and/or organizations to make an agreement by being a means of communication between them.

Guard

Guarding one's own interest is the ultimate aim of successful foe management. Basic to any management principle is the idea to get the best deal out of any given situation. Accordingly, in managing malevolent peers, one should always keep this in mind. Yet to be very frank, one should not only guard one's interest zealously but also watch out for encroachment. While encroaching upon others' sphere of influence or interest, one should always have the preparedness to counter any malignant overture on the part of the enemy.

Negotiate

In the no-win situation, it is prudent to negotiate. Negotiation is a policy best adopted when one is trying to gain some ground in any field vis-a-vis an able competitor. It can take place prior to a showdown, or in between a show down or after a clash of interest. In our present time, both in the political and the economic fields, we come across the negotiation process not only to form a government but also to settle wages and compensation.

Since foe management starts with the presumption that there are areas of disagreement and clash of interest, it is essential not only to take the help of an able negotiator but also to be aware of the latest trends and nuances of the same skill.

FORGIVE

Forgive is the word that mostly sounds anathema if used in the context of foe management. But from the example of

Sri Krishna's life, we know that the capability to forgive the foe for some limited time is a desirable trait in a manager/leader, though forgetting an act of malevolence is not always advisable.

The word FORGIVE collectively stands for

F —Forgive

O—Obstruct

R—Remember

G—Gather

I —Ignore

V—Visualize

E—Entangle

Forgive

Forgiving the enemy is a virtue rarely exhibited and understood even by the best peer-managers. Forgiveness is generally considered to be a sign of meekness and weakness. The general belief and misconception is that one forgives either when pushed to the corner as a gesture of helplessness and surrender, or when one's own kith and kin are involved. Of course, we derive our lesson from the behaviour of our role model Sri Krishna. By forgiving Sishupala under circumstances other than those quoted above, he had established that forgiveness is one of the most powerful tools of foe management, which if used correctly gives good dividends in terms of public image.

After giving it a fair try, one can revert to harsher methods of do or die.

Obstruction

A timely and well-designed obstruction helps greatly in pre-emptive damage-control exercises. Obstruction and observation being the twin objectives of a malevolent peer, one should always be extra alert to foresee the events and the situation that may result in wrongful loss to self and wrongful gain to the enemy. While working the way out and strengthening preventive measures, one should not hesitate to resort to quid-pro-quo.

In fact, if the selfish and evil designs of the enemy were not countered in time, it would not be long before one finds oneself absolutely obscured and neck deep in trouble. Besides, if one does no work on offensive obstructions, then the enemy may get bolder and stronger. Offensive obstructions are the checkmates of chess that remind the enemy that it is being watched and may get trapped too in its own net.

Remember

Forgetting any single lesson of history is the worst thing to do in foe management. Hence one must make it a point to remember every adventure as well as misadventure of the enemy.

FORGIVE

but

do not

FORGET.

While it is prudent to forgive the enemy at times, it is never prudent to forget the events and the lessons learnt. Because this equals to giving the other camp another chance for repeating the misadventure at one's own cost.

Besides one should also remember each and every strategy and tactic adopted by the enemy on every occasion. It is like knowing your opponents' positive and negative points and making the best use of the knowledge.

In fact, not only should one remember the acts of omission and commission on the part of the enemy but also should learn from the life experience of the others, i.e., from the similarly situated people.

Gather

Gathering information about the foe and collecting the enemies' enemies together under one's own umbrella ensures one's own victory even in the most difficult situations.

Human civilization having evolved from the hunter and gatherer stage of primitive economy has always carried the tell tale mark of hoarding and accumulating. All our enmity is based on instinctive competition and greed for a bigger hoarding. In that pursuit, we need to defend ourselves, counter the others' move, not only to survive, but also to ensure lasting deterrence. One gets a higher percentage of success if one gathers as much information about the other party as possible. Additional bonus is ensured if the enemies' enemy joins our own endeavour too.

Ignore

At times, ignoring the pinpricks prevents the escalation of a head-on clash. Since foes are foes because of clash of interest and ideology, it is but natural that the other side would like to gauge the strength and to create minor irritants at one time or the other. Though it is advisable to take note of it, it is prudent to handle it in a casual manner as far as possible and avoid blowing it out of proportion in public. Especially in propaganda war, it is absolutely prudent to watch and ignore for some time before reacting and responding.

It is also advisable because sometimes the opposite camp tries to exhaust the enemy by engaging in minor irritants. Such irritants are also used as distractions when actually some long-scale offence is planned at some other front. So a cautious approach is required.

Visualization

Without visualizing the enemies' next and future steps, one can't hope to gain an upper hand.

Not only is it very essential to keep track of internal changes and probable competitions from within the enemy camp so as to plan one's own defence and victory, but it is also very essential to update the contingency plan.

In spiritual sciences, "visualization" is a word that is used to strengthen one's own will power. But this is a very powerful tool in every aspect of management. Visualization of market trends, supporters' sentiment, climatic conditions, technological changes, political waves, etc. is a must if one wants to master the art and science of foe-management.

Entangle

While entangling the enemy in a cobweb of wisely spread network, one should take care to avoid self-entanglement.

Entanglement is the worst way of wasting energy, time, resources, and emotions in a tricky situation. Most of the time, it leads one nowhere and the net result is a big zero. So, one should know how to use it to one's own advantage and apply it on the enemy to keep the enemy's attention diverted.

Entanglement in war of prices (in market economy), in long-drawn political war, in sibling rivalry, in the affairs of heart, etc., which do not result in positive outcome over a period of definable time, are not worth sustaining. One should guard against it while using it as a weapon to keep the other camp preoccupied.

THE CHAMELEONS AND THE FENCE SITTERS: THE INDIFFERENT PEERS

Like the events of life the peers whether benevolent or malevolent, don't always fall into water-tight compartments. Some of our peers are at times benevolent and at other times malevolent. Some of them can be won over with some effort to our camp and some tend to cross over to the other camp. They are like the chameleons and double-edged swords who need special handling and separate treatment. However the fence sitters are the indifferent lot who generally believe in minding their own business until and unless circumstances and eventuality pull them into centre stage. They carry the burden of benevolent or malevolent peership only when it is thrust upon them and they are willing to be a party to it.

THE CHAMELEONS

Changing the colour of the exterior skin as per the external surroundings does help in evading the predator's alert eyes. When the lizard does it, it does so for its self-protection. In fact, it is an asset, which is extremely prized in foe management. But the flip side of it is that the enemy's agents and the fence sitters from within one's own camp might as well be using it too for their own benefit. So one has to carefully watch out.

The Chameleons can be categorized under three groups (1) the enemy agents or malevolent chameleons (2) the inimical friends of the self or benevolent chameleons (3) The inimical friends of the enemy. Before we study their characteristic traits, let us understand why the chameleons are the chameleons and recount the events from the life of our role model Sri Krishna.

THE CHAMELEONS VIS-A-VIS SRI KRISHNA

Like any other human being of his stature, Sri Krishna was born and brought up among people who were actually no match for him. And being a leader, he was ahead of his time and much above the petty mind of his contemporaries. Nonetheless the dwarfs in any time and clime find it difficult to accept such a personality. They may or may not exhibit their antagonism openly yet all the while they think ill of the person and look for opportunities to embarrass without getting caught.

In fact, it is very difficult to expose the chameleons. And another impossible thing is to visualize their next movement.

Anyway from the consequences of certain acts and facts some tale-tell signs can be counted to fortify one's own fort and to take preventive measures.

In the early life of Sri Krishna, when he was taken to Gopapura from Mathura and left under the guardianship of Nandas, several attempts were made on his life by the secret agents of Kamsa. Some of these agents were known as Aghasura, Vakasura, Putana, etc. The male agents like Aghasura and Vakasura came in the disguise of cowherd playmates and tried fatal tricks. Putana, the female agent, came as a lactating woman and tried to kill him while breastfeeding. Though it was said that the supernatural powers and awakened Kundalini protected Sri Krishna, other factors and common sense indicate that alertness on the part of friendly and well meaning elders did facilitate effective countering of the attempts.

From the very fact that enemy agents could trace his secret place of hiding, it is clear that some people from the inner circle of his foster parents must have leaked out the information. Though we don't know who those faceless yet harmful chameleons from within the camp were, it is certain that they did exist. Otherwise if his parents could smuggle him out of the dungeon by hoodwinking the royal staff, how could it be possible that the enemy could find out the safe house?

However, it is also a fact that not only during his childhood but also thereafter Sri Krishna survived many attempts on his life. Most of it was rendered ineffective due to good networking and tapping of the goodwill of the enemy's inimical friends. Again for prudence's sake, these names were kept as highly guarded secrets, yet such benevolent elements did exist.

The Traits of the Chameleons

Now let us analyse the traits of the chameleons both the malevolent and the benevolent ones.

- They are elusive.
- They keep a low profile and pretend to be one from the own camp.
- They are deceitful.
- They are goal-oriented but have a soft and pretentious exterior.

❀ They are good at laying traps for the others.

❀ If unchecked and uncountered, they take undue advantage of the situation for furthering their cause.

❀ Being very dedicated and skillful, they pass through the weak links in the defense mechanism and they strike from within.

❀ When malevolent, they are more dangerous than the pronounced and known enemy.

❀ When benevolent, they are more effective than the die-hard friends.

❀ They don't take things for granted.

❀ They are good executives.

❀ They are thorough and have a professional approach towards their objective.

❀ They need enough compensation to undertake any risk.

❀ Being acutely aware of the risk, they invite it upon themselves, and are extremely adventurous.

❀ Their loyalty and dedication towards their objective is beyond doubt.

❀ Being faceless, they don't crave for fame and popularity.

❀ They don't inspire mass following but are highly prized by their benefactors.

CHAMELEONS

* Elusive
* Deceitful
* Good executives
* Soft and pretentious exterior
* Goal-oriented
* Very dangerous (malevolent ones)
* Very effective (benevolent ones)
* Loyal, dedicated and skilful
* Less sociable and lack showmanship
* Silent workers and silent killers

They are the double-edged swords and are difficult to tackle through direct confrontation and fight.

❀ They lack showmanship and are less sociable.

❀ Their expectations from life, self and others are not very high.

❀ They neither have any complexes nor do they suffer from any hangover or guilt conscience.

❀ They mean business.

❀ They lack sense of humour and treat life as a practical joke.

❀ They come and go without fanfare and mourning.

❀ But they do inspire like-minded people.

❀ They are silent workers and silent killers.

❀ They believe in lying low and striking at the opportune time.

MANAGEMENT TOOLS OF KRISHNA

Sri Krishna and his benevolent peers used the traditional tools of administration, i.e., Sama, Dana, Danda, and Bheda. The faceless and camouflaged enemy in waiting is difficult to tackle through direct methods of confrontation and fight. In fact, action can be taken only when one detects their presence and their exact intention is known.

To identify and understand the chameleon, one has to initially use Bheda, Dana and Sama. Bheda traditionally meant intelligence and breach. Breaching the confidence and secrets of the chameleon's exterior is the toughest preventive as well as the best defensive measure, which allows one to gain access to the enemy's mind. And collecting intelligence or encouraging the chameleon to spill the information, strengthens one's position further.

Dana stands both for bribe and compensation/reward. It exploits the greed of the recipient's mind. Usually the chameleons accept the job either for an ideological/ emotional reason or to settle a score or to gain something. The gain could be anything and everything. The persuader has to find the temptation or the emotional hangovers that motivate the chameleon, and has to isolate it from other factors so as to cultivate on the very same ground. However, if there is a score to settle, the wise, either try to play it down or allow a minor settling at their own expense in order to neutralize the mental hostility. Dana is supposed to be the most effective tool.

Sama of course means good counselling or negotiation through talk or discussion. It could be handled directly or through a mediator. It is used discreetly to win over the chameleons from within one's own camp and in the camp of the enemy's inimical friends. By interpreting and projecting the facts in a different manner and from a different angle, these unpredictable chameleons can be persuaded to cooperate. In fact "Sama" in this context actually means effective persuasion.

In fact, throughout his life, Sri Krishna had always exhibited immense patience and tact in handling the known and unknown chameleons. So much so that at times it surprised both his friends and foes. However, he never allowed himself to be pushed around and went by his own conviction. The height of his experimentation with his own inner conviction was seen during the famous Mahabharata war when he exhorted Arjuna to fight the war yet at the same time persuaded (Yudhisthira) to seek the blessings from the elders. By seeking their blessing, their goodwill was won over and their hostility was softened. Thus a huge pocket of hidden well-wishers was created.

MODERN MANAGEMENT PRINCIPLES

For our own purpose, suiting to our own time and clime, we may reinvent the traditional concepts and their dimensions as Investigation, Compensation, Persuasion and Extermination.

Investigation

There are certain misconceptions about the word investigation which is generally understood as a follow up action to find the truth once an event takes place. But, in reality, nothing could be farthest from the truth. For, investigation should start even before the events take place. It should be anticipatory to check the state of affairs and to detect the existence of the chameleons if any. But it should be kept discreet and absolutely confidential.

Compensation

Once the real state of affairs is known and the actions as well as motives are clear, it is essential to find out the requirement and temptations of the person or the persons involved. The enticement of riches or any other favour both in terms of cash and kind has to be worked out either to demotivate the person from executing the task or to motivate them to go ahead.

Persuasion

There are people who are misled to believe in certain misconstrued facts, on the basis of which they decide to take the responsibility of the chameleon (it could be imposed by other or could be self-imposed). These people can be dissuaded as well as persuaded to change camp by mere counselling, supported by hard and straight facts. But they are to be always taken with a pinch of salt because they are by nature prone to getting influenced.

Extermination

All the three, combined and applied with due discretion and consideration, can yield desired results. However, in extreme cases, one has to resort to extermination without any mercy. This is Danda in classical terms, but does not necessarily mean punishment. "Danda" is punitive by nature. "Extermination" is an assertive/offensive self-defence. It also sends a specific and decisive message to the enemy.

Traditional vs. Reinvented Tools

Traditional	Reinvented
Bheda	Investigation
Dana	Compensation
Sama	Persuasion
Danda	Extermination

Besides, the fear of extermination can also be used to get the effect of counselling.

THE FENCE SITTERS: THE INDIFFERENT PEERS

Before we proceed to study this group and the management tools, let us first understand the distinction between a Chameleon and a fence sitter. A Chameleon as we know is a tool of hidden agenda, who believes in hiding the intentions and even its own existence to facilitate the objective. However, a fence sitter is like the Humpty Dumpty who prefers to sit on a wall and often ends up in a great fall. Unable to make up his/her mind, the fence sitter prefers to tread the middle path but is always ready to change the track in favour of one or the other. They try to remain neutral, but more often than not they tend to be partial. But they prefer to keep it to themselves without exhibiting any outward symptoms till such time they decide to take a side.

So, fence sitters become somewhat known, while the chameleons remain faceless. The fence sitters are neither malevolent nor benevolent but have the capacities to be either of them; whereas the chameleons being chameleons are definitely either malevolent or benevolent. They can also be used as double-edged weapons. This makes the chameleons more dangerous than the fence sitters.

FENCE SITTER

is like the

Humpty Dumpty

who prefers

to sit on a wall

and often

ends up in a

great fall.

Chameleons	Fence sitters
Remain faceless	Known figure
Either malevolent or benevolent	Indifferent
Double-edged weapons	Simple, naive and non-ambitious
Loyal and dedicated	Neither loyal nor disloyal

THE FENCE SITTERS VIS-A-VIS SRI KRISHNA

In fact, when we talk of personalities like Sri Krishna, it is the common man and woman who behave like the fence sitter. Though simple, naive and non-ambitious, these people matter a lot either in resisting or in facilitating any change in centre of power. Mostly skeptical, they however live with an innate understanding that irrespective of their existence, likes or dislikes, somebody or other would be required to manage one or the other form of collective socio-economic-political affairs of public life. Though in the conflict of interest, it is they who pay heavily in the form of dislocation and labour, yet they are neither loyal nor disloyal to any particular individual. They simply give a chance to everybody and try their own patience in the form of passive or active support.

The people of Mathura and Yadava republican confederacies tolerated Kamsa as long as he could hold on his own. When time and tide changed in favour of Sri Krishna, they welcomed him and celebrated his victory. Kamsa was relegated to the dustbin of disdain and discredit.

Apart from the public, it is the media which also acts like a fence sitter but with a third dimension. It moulds the public opinion by feeding the rumour mill, providing information and suggesting perceived positive or negative impacts of a future event. It also takes upon itself the responsibility of a self-appointed watchdog and intelligence agency on behalf of the public. So, naturally both the public and the media complement and supplement each other.

In the case of Sri Krishna, it was the media, which created hype against Kamsa even before Sri Krishna was conceived and born. And after his birth, it worked over time fuelling the imagination and swaying the mind of the public as well as that of the enemy. It was partial in this case. But once Kamsa was removed from the scene, the media simply lost its role and did not know what to do.

Apart from the public and media, there are specific personalities whose fence sitting does affect decision-making. In Sri Krishna's case, when he was deciding in favour of Pandava brothers, one fence sitter, loomed large on the horizon. He was namely Balarama, Sri Krishna's elder brother. Duryodhana was absolutely conscious of Sri Krishna's assets and powers. So he always tried to keep his elder brother, i.e., Balarama in good humour. He even formally enrolled as his student and learnt the art and science of mace fight from him. So much so that when he went to Sri Krishna seeking his alliance and assistance for Mahabharata war, Balarama was unhappy with Sri Krishna for taking the side of Pandavas. So he decided to remain neutral and set out for spiritual tourism. He came back only on the last day of the great war and was quite annoyed with Sri Krishna for encouraging Bhima to break the rules of mace war and incapacitate Duryodhana by breaking his thighs.

Now let us list out the traits of the fence sitters.

Characteristic Traits of the Fence Sitters

❀ The fence sitters are famous for their wait and watch policy.

❀ They are conscious of their own interest and don't bother much about the conflicting parties.

❀ They harbour neither grouse nor any complex.

❀ They do inspire their own following.

❀ They are skilful and experts in their own field.

❀ The fence sitters are ambitious in their own way.

❀ They are very good at mediation if at all their services are used for the purpose.

❀ Being independent and balanced by nature they are not very emotional.

❀ They are the bullies who are better left alone.

❀ If they see red and once aroused from their complacence, they may cause havoc.

❀ They are prone to big falls due to their foolhardiness.

FENCE SITTERS

* Independent
* Wannabe
* Egocentric
* Self-righteous
* Wait and watch policy
* Good negotiators
* Selfish
* Prone to big falls
* Indifferent

Power to survive dominates in all deeds.

MANAGEMENT TOOLS

Being ahead of his time and extraordinarily gifted, Sri Krishna was intelligent enough to see through the strength and weaknesses of his friends, foes, chameleons as well as that of the fence sitters. With the fence sitters, he was diplomatic enough to pamper their ego and thereby encourage them to keep a safe distance. Wherever required he used the Sama, Bheda and Dana but rarely used Danda.

Sama or advice helped in making the fence sitters stick to their middle path. Bheda or intelligence collection kept one well informed about the real intention of the fence sitters. Dana or support at the time of need without putting any string for return favour helped in keeping them in good humour.

It was almost like handling a non-aligned nation. Like the non-aligned nations, the fence sitters are neither the superpowers nor the underprivileged. Though lacking the clout of the superpowers and being above the miseries of the underprivileged, they are somehow regarded as the wannabes who are worth watching. Because of their potential for growth, they also form the potential group of allies of the unforeseen future if cultivated properly. Similarly, in the market economy, they have the power to swing the balance in somebody or others favour.

Due to their selfish desires and wavering mind at times, the fence sitters make their own position very precarious like the proverbial Humpty Dumpty. And when they fall they take time to recover, at times too long. But it is never wise to stage-manage their fall, rather it is advisable to let them continue in their stance and if possible pamper their ego. In the minds of the public, they project a strange image of proud impartials, who if need be, can provide alternative leadership. In fact, this is what most of the fence sitters keep waiting for. It is not that they are all naive and simpletons. But the image of theirs is that of the "self-respecting proud poor thing".

Beneath the cover of dignified indifference they are extremely self righteous and judgmental. The right approach towards these people is to keep them at the right distance and at the right place. In fact, it won't hurt much to keep them obliged. Because their tacit loyalty is more powerful than that of any tested ally.

DYNAMICS OF PEER MANAGEMENT

In the preceding chapters, we have learnt about the hypotheses derived from the life story of Sri Krishna and have developed the principles suitable to our time and clime. In this section, we will acquaint ourselves with the utility value of peer management and its dynamics vis-a-vis different real-life situations.

Since the peer group associations form a major source of influence and pressure tactics in the decision-making process (in the life of both individual as well as organization and society), it is very essential to understand the dynamics of the interactive forces of peer management. So it is but logical to have some idea about the role of various forces.

Peers operate within a system which is subject to both change and status quo, conflict and entente, gain and loss, competition and camaraderie.

PEER MANAGEMENT SKILLS VIS-A-VIS ORGANIZATIONAL GOAL

The word organization here is a comprehensive one that includes socio-economic, political, cultural and interpersonal aspects of life wherein some kind of a hierarchy is followed.

In general, the broad organizational goals and objectives are better output, enhanced financial gain, sustained growth, healthy intra-organizational movement, successful competition in the operating field, healthy public as well as private image, etc. All these organizational goals are achieved by various intra-organizational teams. These teams are nothing but different forms of peer groups working within their specific subsystems. A proper co-ordination between these subsystems, and between the players and their interaction with dynamic forces act as that 'X' factor which draws the dividing line between failure, success and excellence. If we plot it graphically, the net result of interaction between peer management and organizational goals would look like the following graph.

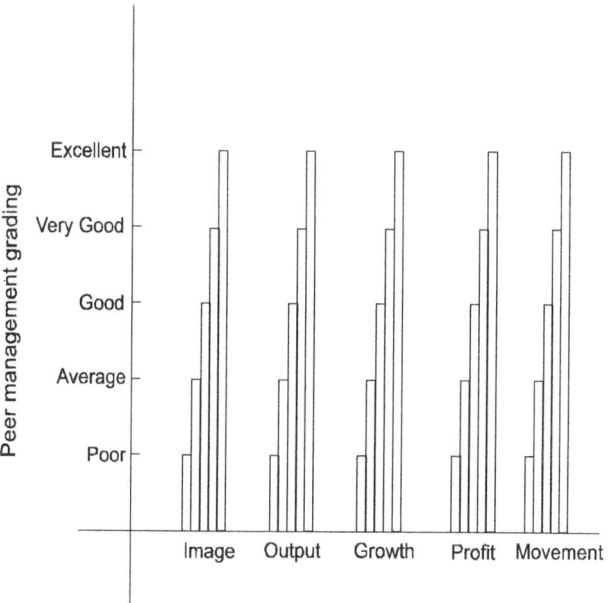

Organizational goals (Graph - I)

In a healthy and excellent organizational atmosphere where healthy peer management prevails, the organizational goals gradually escalate. However, unhealthy and diminishing gradation of peer management results in gradual diminishing of the net achievement of organizational goal. A combination of different gradation for different organizational goals creates a variegated graph of organizational achievements: as represented in Graph II.

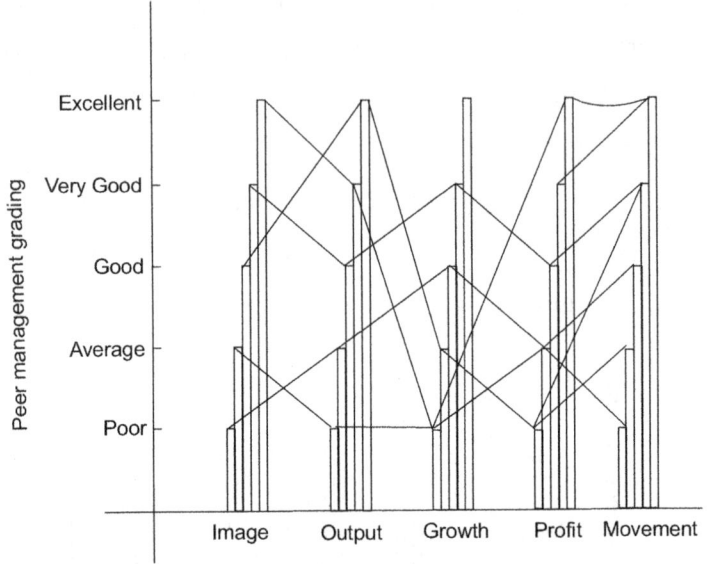

Organizational goals (Graph-II)

In fact the HRD managers do little to go deep into the dynamics of peer management and its impact on the overall organizational goal and growth. For our own benefit, let us use a concentric double pentagon to understand the interactive forces and their impact on both peer management and organizational goals.

The cross currents arising out of different arms of the concentric double pentagons make or mar the present and future prospects of both the organization as well as the players.

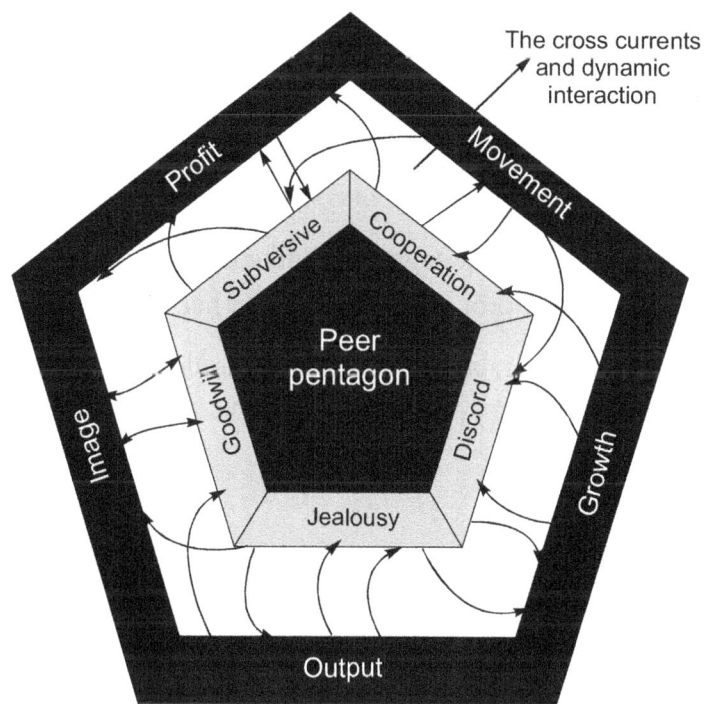

Organizational concentric double pentagon

PEER MANAGEMENT VIS-A-VIS CONFLICT MANAGEMENT

Conflict is the factor that eventually and if not managed properly results in system breakdown, animosity, and warlike situations. It is a burden on the resource and time. Though conflicts are at times welcomed as a change-inducing factor, it is a big drain on the human resources especially so when there is a fight of the nerve as well as that of interest.

The origin of conflict could be found in real or perceived threats to self-interest, pride, jealousy, grouse, etc. Though there are institutionalized channels to redress the individual grievances, a strong network of benevolent peers and their management helps a lot in containing the situation.

In fact peer management and conflict are both directly and inversely proportional to each other.

If plotted in a graph the chart would look like the one that follows.

(a)

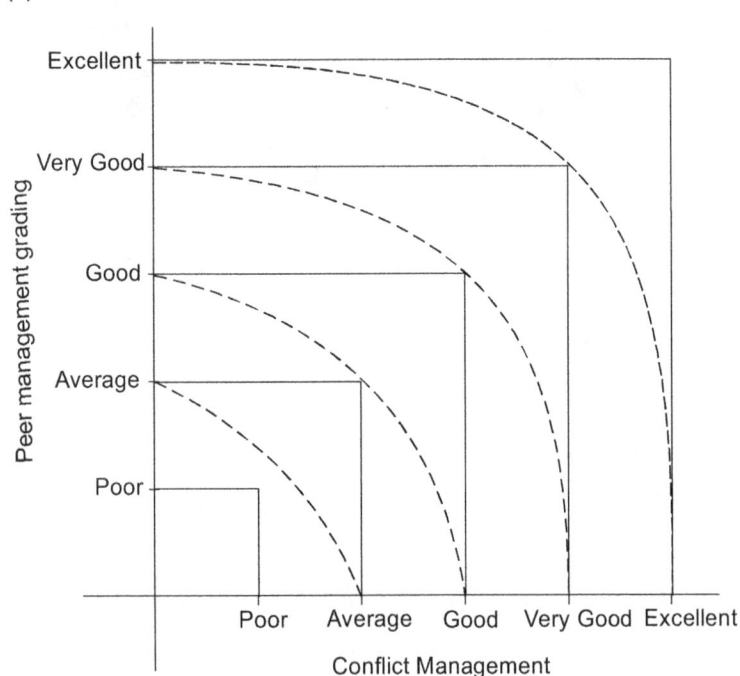

Graph showing directly proportional relationship

The impact of positive peer management is such that it takes conflict management half a step forward in a positive direction if the rating of peer management is higher than that of conflict management.

(b)

Inversely proportional graph

Since conflict is at times, or rather most of the times between the management and workers in an intra-organizational context, and between one organization and the other in a broader context, the peer groups remain separate for both the opposing parties. In the case of intra-group maladjustment, the collective strength gets reduced, thereby reducing the peer pressure to heighten a conflict. In this case, like a weakening low-pressure cyclone, the conflict or the issue of the conflict dies naturally. The conflict gets self-managed or rather smoothened.

PEER MANAGEMENT VIS-A-VIS CHANGE MANAGEMENT

In any system, the ambition and the objectives, whether it is individual or collective, are to carve a better niche for oneself, i.e., trying to make a change, carving a better place, better profit, better security, more power, etc. This change is favourably inclined towards one and so it may be unfavourable towards the others.

The intra-organizational peer-management dynamics, working as a source of positive or negative pressure, has a definite impact on the process of change management. If the peer pressure is positive it results in handling required change in an effective manner thereby achieving sustained growth and surviving the onslaught of changed dynamics of forces from within and without. However, if the peer pressure is negative and destructive, it creates a vacuumlike eerie situation. And since Nature abhors vacuum, it gets filled by whatever material is available in the closed proximity which may or may not be healthy for organizational goals.

In fact the dynamics of change has two different dimensions: (i) intra-organizational (ii) extra-organizational. For the convenience of better understanding, we may call the former as climatic and the latter as environmental. Both the climatic (the changes occurring in and within near proximity), and the environmental (the changes occurring in farther and broader proximity) dynamics of change act upon, get neutralized or moulded by the pressure exerted by the organizational peer groups. This is a very important factor in change management where thoughts are least analysed and most neglected by the higher and middle level leadership. As a result, many organizations grope in darkness wondering why things go wrong despite their best efforts.

The strength of a peer group works either as a cushion or as a gateway in accommodating and managing changes, both positive and negative. Neglect the cushion and the gateway, the motivation, dedication, loyalty, etc. i.e., all soft assets get eroded.

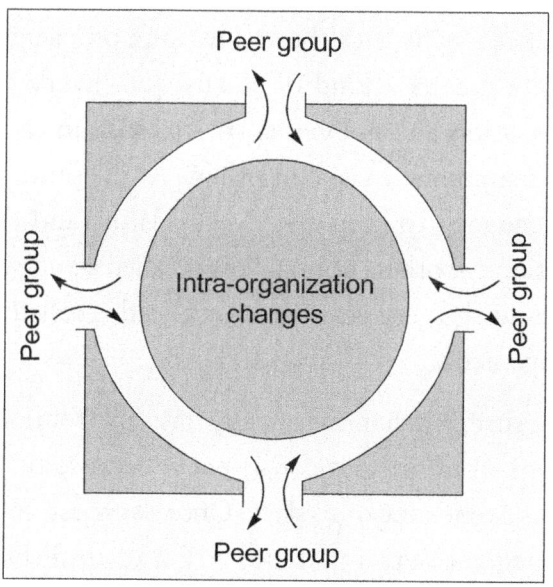

Climatic diagram

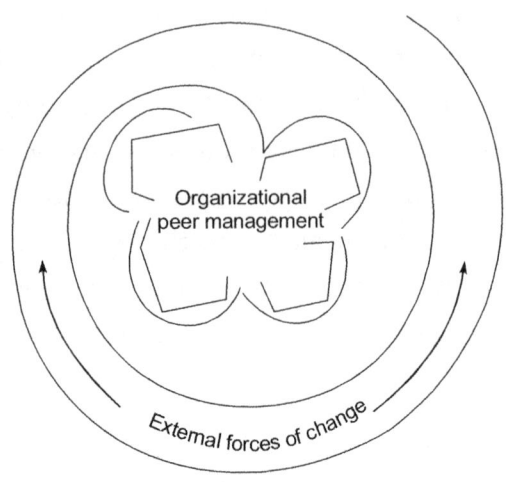

Environment diagram

PEER MANAGEMENT VIS-A-VIS STATUS QUO MANAGEMENT

Existence means both the survival and propagation, which actually means a kind of status quo. Every established organization and individual tries to sustain its own hard-earned supremacy vis-a-vis others. At the same time, there is a tendency to keep other competitors and the nascent ambitions of others at bay. This is called struggle for status quo. And the very effort to stay ahead is called status quo management.

To sustain what one already has, calls for a tremendous amount of effort and consistency. Because once satisfied there is a tendency to go slack. Once slackness, complacency, and neglect sets in, it quickly and quietly eats into enterprising nature and the dynamic forces rust out. It gives the environmental and external change agents a chance to have an upper hand. This tells upon the overall organizational health and goal.

So it is essential for the top and the middle level managers to take frequent stock of the situation and to discourage complacency. Once a target is achieved, a new target should be set and everybody should be motivated to strive for the achievement of the new target and objective.

In fact the best method of status quo management is to rediscover the potential, talent, objective and inspiration. Besides, it needs regular pruning, weeding out, manuring and nurturing but for which the soft and hard assets get weathered.

Here we give a questionnaire to test the strength of peer management dynamics in your organization vis-a-vis the four aspects discussed above as well as to assess your own understanding of the subject. A total of fifty questions under five sub-heads have been given, each carrying two marks for the correct answers, minus two marks for the incorrect answers, and no marks for the questions not answered. A total scoring of more than seventy marks implies healthy peer management dynamics at work. Below sixty marks calls for attention. The answers are given at the end of each questionnaire for calculating the score.

THE QUESTIONNAIRE

Part I—Peer Management Strength Weakness (PMSW)

1. Do you think the worker union is a peer group?

    a) Yes

    a) No

    b) Can't say

    c) Does not exist

2. Do you think an officer's club is a powerful peer group?

    a) Yes

    b) No

    c) To some extent

    d) Can't say

3. Do you think a political party is a layered unstructured peergroup?

    a) Yes

    b) No

    c) Can't say

    d) To some extent

4. Peer management is the most important factor for the survival and growth of the organization.

    a) Not at all

b) Yes, absolutely

c) To some extent

d) Partly, as there are other factors too

5. Peers in the intra-organizational context exert enough pressure to further their self- interest.

a) True

b) False

c) Partly both

d) None

6. Effective peer management has a positive effect on organizational growth.

a) True

b) False

c) Partly both

d) None

7. How does peer management affect change management?

a) Positively

b) Negatively

c) Both ways

d) Neither way

8. Peer management plays an important role in change management.

   a) True

   b) False

   c) Both

   d) Neither

9. Peer management is an asset in sustaining status quo and supremacy.

   a) True

   b) False

   c) Neither

   d) Both

10. Can any organization do away with peer management?

   a) Yes

   b) No

   e) Neither

   f) Both

Answers

1. a   2. b & c   3. a & d   4. d   5. a   6. a

7. c   8. a   9. a   10. a

Part II—Peer Management vis-a-vis Organizational Goal

1. Organizations can survive and grow without any goal.

   a) True

   b) False

   c) both a & b

   d) neither a & b

2. Organizational goals are affected by intra-organizational peer pressure.

   a) True

   b) False

   c) Both a & b

   d) Neither a & b

3. Can the organizational goals be achieved in spite of peer pressure?

   a) Yes

   b) No

   c) To some extent

   d) None

4. The organizational goals are:

   a) Growth

   b) Profit

c) Positive public image

d) All

5. Organizations should encourage healthy competition among the peers.

a) Yes

b) No

c) Can't say

d) None

6. An organization contains many peer groups.

a) True

b) False

c) Neither

d) Both

7. All the peer groups in any organization have similar goals.

a) True

b) False

c) Partly (a) & (b)

d) Neither

8. The intra-organizational peer groups are always structured.

   a) True

   b) False

   c) Both a & b

   d) Neither

9. Positive peer pressure can withstand negative changes.

   a) Yes

   b) No

   c) Partly

   d) Can't say

10. Organizations should do away with peer groups.

    a) Yes

    b) No

    c) Not possible

    d) Can't say

Answers

1. b   2. b   3. c   4. d   5. a   6. a
7. c   8. b   9. both a & c   10. b & c

Part III—Conflict Management vis-a-vis Peer Pressure

1. Conflict is an ideal state of existence

    a) True

    b) False

    c) Neither (a) & (b)

    d) Can't say

2. Conflicts are undesirable.

    a) Yes

    b) No

    c) At times

    d) None

3. Conflicts should be welcomed.

    a) Yes

    b) No

    c) At times

    d) None

4. Conflicts need management

    a) True

    b) False

    c) Partly both (a) & (b)

    d) None

5. Peer pressure is positively proportional to conflict management.

    a) Yes

    b) No

    c) Both a & b

    d) Neither

6. Intra-organizational conflict is a result of poor peer management.

    a) True

    b) False

    c) Partly both (a) & (b)

    d) Neither

7. Intra-organizational conflict should be ignored.

    a) Yes always

    b) No never

    c) At times

    d) Can't say

8. Conflict is avoidable.

    a) Yes

    b) No

    c) At times

    d) None

9. Proper conflict management helps in organizational growth.

   a) True

   b) False

   c) Partly both (a) & (b)

   e) Neither

10. Inter-organizational conflict has nothing to do with peer pressure.

    a) True

    b) false

    c) At times

    d) Can't say

   Answers

   1. b   2. c   3. b & c   4. a   5. c   6. a
   7. c   8. c   9. a   10. c

Part IV—Change Management vis-a-vis Peer Management

1. Change is an essential part of life.

   a) Yes

   b) Not necessarily

   c) No

   d) Neither a, b, c

2. Handling change needs management skills.

    a)   True

    b)   False

    c)   Partly both (a) & (b)

    d)   Neither

3. Change is avoidable.

    a)   Always

    b)   At times

    c)   Never

    d)   Can't say

4. Change management affects organizational goals.

    a)   Yes

    b)   No

    c)   At times

    d)   Never

5. Change management is associated with peer management.

    a)   Totally

    b)   Partly

    c)   Absolutely not

    d)   Can't say

6. Intra-organizational changes are better avoidable as they alter the status quo.

   a) True

   b) False

   c) Both

   d) Neither

7. Extra-organizational change agents should be properly watched and handled.

   a) True

   b) False

   c) Not required

   d) Who cares

8. Peer pressure is one of the change agents.

   a) Yes

   b) No

   c) Both (a) & (b)

   d) Can't say

9. Peer management works as a cushion against change generated shocks.

   a) True

   b) False

   c)   Neither

   d)   Partly both (a) & (b)

10. Change management has both positive and negative effect on peer pressure.

   a)   True

   b)   False

   c)   Neither

   d)   Both

Answers

1. a   2. a   3. b   4. both a & c   5. b
6. b   7. a   8. a   9. a   10. a

Part V—Status quo Management vis a vis Peer Management

1. Maintaining status quo at any cost is the primary objective of organizations.

   a)   True

   b)   False

   c)   Partly true/partly false

   d)   None

2. Status quo management is contradictory to the spirit of peer management.

   a)   True

b)   False

a)   Neither

d)   Both a & b

3.   Peer management sustains status quo maintenance.

a)   True

b)   False

c)   Partly true

d)   Both a & b

4.   Status quo is necessary for organizational stability.

a)   True

b)   False

c)   Partly true

d)   Both a & b

5.   Too much of stress on status quo precedes stagnation.

a)   True

b)   False

c)   Neither (a) & (b)

d)   Partly both (a) & (b)

6.   Peer management has nothing to do with status quo.

a)   True

b) False

c) Partly true

d) Neither

7. Effective status quo management calls for

a) Regular pruning

b) Motivation

c) Job rotation

d) All three

8. Status quo management and peer management go hand in hand.

a) Yes

b) No

c) Neither

d) Can't say

9. Peer management should not ignore the importance of status quo management.

a) True

b) False

c) Neither

d) Both

10. Effective peer management supplements a balanced approach towards status quo and change management.

    a) True

    b) False

    c) Neither

    d) Both

Answers

1. c	2. b	3. c	4. c	5. a	6. b
7. d	8 a	9 a	10. a		

THE DO-S AND DON'T-S OF PEER MANAGEMENT

Like every other branch of behavioural science, peer management too has its do-s and don't-s which need a careful study. In this chapter, we will discuss both these aspects of peer management. We have already stated in the beginning, that the peers are the seers as well as the source of fear. The benevolent peers being privy to intimate and inside details are the potential weak links that can spell disaster if the relationship goes sour. Whereas the malevolent peers being the member of the other side are always at the conflicting interest.

So far, we have discussed how to keep the peers in good humour and at safe distance. Now, we will learn the special caveats vis-a-vis both the friends and the foes. But before we spell the special rules of the game let us first have a look at Sri Krishna's caveats.

DO-S AND DON'T-S OF SRI KRISHNA

Being the most towering and versatile personality of his time, it was but natural that his action as well as inaction would not only draw attention but also inspire thorough analysis and speculation. And these are the two factors that cause fear psychosis, imaginary clash of interest and feed the rumour mill. Intelligent as he was he took extreme care in handling such sensitive matters.

For our better understanding, let us place these do-s and don't-s followed by Sri Krishna under three headings:

1. Organizational

2. Societal

3. Interpersonal

Organizational Do-s and Don't-s

Organizational do-s and don't-s mean the policy adopted vis-a-vis official/position and incumbents of the chairs. Sri Krishna never exhibited lust for power. Neither was he ambitious, otherwise after the death of Kamsa he could have declared himself the king. Though the Yadavas followed the republican principle of succession, Sri Krishna was actually aware of the other eligible aspirants. So, instead of becoming the king, he preferred to become the kingmaker. That was his intra-organizational policy. However, his inter-organizational policy vis-a-vis other players in the field was marked by fierce competition and pragmatism. He followed the principle of war and conquest as and when he felt right. Along with his wit and strategy, he also used his might to wrest victory for himself. But at the same time, he nourished the ambition of his benevolent peers, helped them in getting a better deal in life, stood firm for their cause against all odds, and put everything at stake to prove his commitment. Therefore, amongst the benevolent peers, his policy was live and let live whereas with regard to the foes his policy was victory at any cost.

Societal Do-s and Don't-s

In spite of being a very sociable and colourful man, Sri Krishna was an out and out rebel. In societal context, he lived the life as per his will and set his own terms and conditions. As an all-rounder, he had mastered the art and science of healing, killing, entertaining and counselling. He had fully developed his physical, mental, spiritual, scientific, cultural and emotional potentials to the fullest capabilities.

He used all his skills as per the situational requirement of space and time. As a master charmer, he charmed his way into the heart of his benevolent peers. None of his foes were any match for his skills. Though he followed a certain code of conduct of his own his approach was basically amoral and non-conformist. He broke many an existing societal mores and created new ones.

Interpersonal Do-s and Don't-s

Sri Krishna, an enlightened soul, believed in intense and committed interpersonal relationship and he lived his belief. His personal relationships were selective and exclusive. But those who were lucky enough to be included in that list enjoyed his peerage for the lifetime.

However, he never allowed anybody to take him for granted, nor did he himself take anybody for granted. All his foes and friends were made to respect him both from a distance as well as from close proximity. When his magnanimity was slightly disrespected, he did not hesitate to teach the unworthy a quick but effective lesson. At the same time, he did not leave any stone unturned when his protegee needed his attention. We all know the story of

Draupadi's humiliation and the subsequent mode of revenge. We have read about Sudama the poor and the act of bountiful magnanimity. We know of Arjuna's moments of trial and turbulence that gave us the Srimad Bhagavat Gita.

MODERN VERSIONS OF THE DO-S AND DON'T-S

Now let us codify the do-s and don't-s in our contemporary terminology. But before we go ahead, let us remind ourselves that in peer management, these "dos and don'ts" occupy a very important place because of their utility value vis-a-vis change management, conflict management, crisis as well as disaster and status quo management.

ORGANIZATIONAL DO-S AND DON'T-S

1. Don't exhibit your own ambition. Keep it a guarded secret.

2. Do respect others' ambition.

3. Don't join the rush for the top slot. Instead bide your time.

4. Do give a stiff competition to the competitors in your interorganizational set-up.

5. Do learn to hold your own and to swim against the current, while swimming in the organizational crosscurrents.

6. Do allow others a place of their own under the sun.

7. Do allow the grass to grow under the shade but keep them well pruned within their limits.

8. Do remember that your self-interest is as sacrosanct as collective interest.

9. Do remember nothing succeeds like success.

SOCIETAL DO-S AND DON'T-S

1. Do avoid competition with your benevolent peers.

2. Do have a non-judgmental attitude that helps you a lot.

3. In the matter of marital alliances, the equation gets both strengthened as well as weakened by proper or improper handling of the benevolent and malevolent peers.

4. Measured interaction is a must to sustain and derive benefits.

5. Do not encourage too much of interference.

6. Do share the information on the need-to-know basis to avoid unwanted surprises from the chameleons and the fence sitters.

7. Do give without any expectation on return.

8. Do avoid public denouncement of any oversight or lapse.

9. Do forgive but don't forget.

10. Do cultivate, prune and nurture as per time, place and event.

INTERPERSONAL DO-S AND DON'T-S

1. Do test the thought, belief, word and action of the peers again and again.

2. Don't forget to take note of the pattern, while allowing margin for individual idiosyncrasies.

3. Do avoid clashes of interest with benevolent peers.

4. Do allow some escape routes to avoid rebound effects, while bashing a foe.

5. Never trash a benevolent peer either in public or in private.

6. Do care and share because sharing and caring as per the need helps one rise above the petty mentality and establishes one as a leader.

7. Never let anybody be privy to one's private and secret aspects of life.

8. Don't reveal all your assets.

9. Do have a fallback strategy for hard tims.

10. Don't hesitate to lend the shoulder when the peers (benevolent) need to cry.

11. Do manage the interpersonal relationships rising above emotions and illusions.

12. Don't hesitate to call a spade a spade if required.

In fact, apart from all these riders, what matters is the judicious exercise of prudence and common sense as per time, place and situation. A small mistake in sensing the difference at times blows things out of proportion and causes irreparable damage to many a relationship.

EPILOGUE

To translate any hypothetical learning into a reality, one has to understand the matter first in the context of models and hypothetical case studies. The effective gain of this knowledge also needs to be practised either in a dummy situation or through peer management games.

This has to be arranged by the HRD department of individual organizations. However, in the case of individual human beings, one needs to keep in mind the wisdom and symbols spelt out in the book so as to apply those in real-life situations. Besides, one must supplement from one's own experience and must use experiences as vitamins to keep one's peer management skills in good health. It will be worthwhile to remember that both the flute and discus of Sri Krishna stood respectively for the symbols of benevolent and malevolent peer management. Though in our real life, none of us use these two items, the symbolic value of these two instruments; i.e., flute for power of effective and wise use of speech and discus for emotions, will power and action, must always be kept in mind in order to avoid a rigid and fixed mind approach towards the events of life.

Life is a dynamic flowing so is peer management. A prudent and practical approach towards peer management is a vital component of successful and dynamic life management.

Though none of us had the formal grooming for handling friends and foes in the most ideal manner, all of us learnt some tricks from the school of life. At different places, under different circumstances, and in the company of different people, we did pick up some cues here and there. The folklores, stories from the lives of other eminent and not-so-eminent people, incidents from our own life and from the lives of people in our known circle gave us the required input on the basis of which we created our own models of behaviour without ever critically analysing the facts and figures.

Whether we like it or not, life and its various situations need varied management skills to tell a successful story. And managers can be groomed, as management skills can be mastered by anybody who is willing to do so if one remembers that patience and perseverance are the watchwords, and practice is the mother of all skills.

Those who practise dexterous peer management skills have nothing to lose, but gain a whole world of success, goodwill and growth. Do give it a try and we can exchange notes to further enrich our life-management skills.

Made in the USA
Monee, IL
07 July 2026

56552363R00138